LEARNER CONTROLLED INSTRUCTION

The Instructional Design Library

Volume 26

LEARNER CONTROLLED INSTRUCTION

Frank T. Wydra

Harper-Grace Hospitals, Detroit

Danny G. Langdon
Series Editor

Educational Technology Publications
Englewood Cliffs, New Jersey 07632

Library of Congress Cataloging in Publication Data

Wydra, Frank T
    Learner controlled instruction.

    (The Instructional design library; v. 26)
    Bibliography: p.
    1. Programmed instruction. 2. Individualized
instruction. 3. Audio-visual education. I. Title.
II. Series: Instructional design library; v. 26.
LB1028.5.W9   371.39'442   79-23017
ISBN 0-87778-146-X

Printed in the United States of America.

Library of Congress Catalog Card Number:
79-23017.

International Standard Book Number:
0-87778-146-X.

First Printing: March, 1980.

FOREWORD

Learner Controlled Instruction is one of my favorite strategies for effective and efficient instruction. It not only promotes many positive outcomes for students, but it also produces cost benefits that have made users most enthusiastic about its utility. This is not to say, of course, that it has universal application, but where appropriately matched to needs and learning environment, it *really works!*

My first introduction to LCI was as a project director in charge of a team of instructional technologists and subject specialists in redesigning a training program for bank managers in a leading banking concern. This design provided an effective delivery system for on-the-job students to learn skills, and it promoted many of the affective qualities we often seek in learning but generally leave to chance. LCI allows the students to make these things happen, rather than standing in their way. The reader may wonder how this is so from the rather simplified manner in which it is structured. Freedom to choose when, where, and what—rather than being locked into a pattern of doing as chosen by others—provides strong incentives to doing a job well. This is no less true in the process of learning.

Danny G. Langdon
Series Editor

PREFACE

The contents of this book have emerged from the creative genius of hundreds of learners who demonstrated their capacity to overcome the constraints imposed upon them by instructional designers. They showed that they were self-reliant enough to make decisions that were seldom delegated to them. They made those decisions responsibly and in ways that aided in the training of designers, including the author. The processes described herein can be attributed to a number of competent instructional designers who refused to say in advance that all of their decisions were right. Instead they insisted on *validation.* And, indeed, many times their skepticism was justified. Foremost among these designers are Ronald J. Rivers, Frank A. Seaver, III, Erica J. Keeps, and Harry Lebovitz. They made Learner Controlled Instruction a reality.

Credit must also go to a number of people who greatly influenced the process of writing this book. Danny G. Langdon, Series Editor, insisted upon production, relevance, and timeliness. Without his prodding, little would have been done. Jane Raitt labored through the drafts and pointed out inconsistencies in both style and logic. Her advice was valued and applied. Finally, and perhaps most importantly, was the help of Jackie McClure, who suffered through a half dozen drafts, patiently and professionally tolerating revision upon revision. Without her deep regard for deadlines, Learner Controlled Instruction would still be an experience worth writing about some day.

F.T.W.

CONTENTS

ABSTRACT

LEARNER CONTROLLED INSTRUCTION

Learner Controlled Instruction (LCI) is an instructional strategy that allows key learning decisions to be made by the learner, rather than by the instructor. Some such decisions are pace, sequence, content, and evaluation of instruction. LCI also provides a framework for incorporating a variety of instructional tactics, such as audio instruction, video instruction, or programmed instruction, into a program that most efficiently achieves the learning objective. Efficiency is gained through individualization which, in turn, allows utilization of prior learning and unique learning patterns. However, it is when LCI is used with large populations that its economic impact is most significant. The economics are derived from reduction of learning time and by shifting the expenditures to fixed resources from instructional labor.

The application of LCI is flexible. It can be used in group or individual settings. But this flexibility requires a consistent attention to detail and a thorough knowledge of the consequences of actions in the learning environment. The designer, utilizing LCI, will be defining learning outcomes and will be pairing short-term consequences to them. The outcomes paired with predictable consequences provide overall control of the learning program, even though individual decisions are delegated.

Construction of an LCI program involves extensive definition. The designer is responsible for defining the learning mission, population characteristics, required performance results, and environmental specifications, including all assumptions and theories. Learning experiences are then constructed to incorporate a statement of objectives, a definition of performance measurements, and an identification of learning resources. Finally, the design is validated and the program packaged. As can be seen, the instructional effort is invested in design rather than application. The result is a program where key decisions can be delegated to the learner, while the designer has assurances that the desired learning will be achieved.

LEARNER CONTROLLED INSTRUCTION

I.

INTRODUCTION

Learner Controlled Instruction (LCI) is a mode of instruction in which one or more key instructional decisions are delegated to the learner. Some of these decisions include pacing, sequencing, resource accessing, and even evaluation. Learner Controlled Instruction is sometimes confused with Individualized Instruction. While all LCI is individualized, not all individualized instruction is learner controlled. For example, tutoring or individualized coaching is presented on a one-to-one basis and is, therefore, individualized. The individual responses of the learner are evaluated by the instructor or coach. These forms of instruction are tightly controlled by the instructor and are, therefore, *not Learner* Controlled Instruction.

The Learner Controlled Instruction model, however, does not demand that *all* decisions be made by the learner. The instructional strategist may decide to delegate sequencing and resource accessing to the learner while retaining control of objectives and evaluations; or, the evaluation may be delegated, but the sequencing required to reach the objective may be controlled. In either case, the result is a form of Learner Controlled Instruction.

If these definitions were followed to their extremes, one could easily make a case for all instruction being classified as learner controlled. For example, it could be argued that the design error that restricted the learner's control over his or her movements. We did not manage the environment. The resource that was made available to the learner gained control over the learner's ability to move freely and, therefore, altered the nature of the instruction. The controlled environment, its management, and the learner's freedom of movement will all be explored at greater length in the following pages. For now, though, it is necessary to emphasize the point that LCI is not learner anarchy. There *is* control. But it is on the environmental level. There *is* direction. But it is a function of the design of the environment. There *is* learner freedom. But it is within the consequences and resources that have been built into the environment.

The movement toward the development of the LCI instructional mode is an outgrowth of many forces. The first among these is the increasing perishability of our knowledge. A half century ago, Alfred North Whitehead (1929) commented that, for the first time in the history of mankind, what was learned in childhood was not sufficient to sustain a person throughout a lifetime. Some recent projections note that our knowledge doubles each decade. This accelerating explosion of knowledge requires that we design new, more efficient learning systems that will effectively and economically allow for initial and continuing education. Strong forces, however, work against the development of such systems. George Leonard (1968) has said that preventing change in any deep or significant way is precisely what most societies require of their educators. In 1971, a task force reported to the then Secretary of Health, Education, and Welfare, Eliot Richardson, that the graduate schools had become steadily more inner-directed and less responsive to the needs of society. These expressions highlight the care that must be taken with the introduction of new instructional models. The need for change must be present. The existing educational models have produced cultures and individuals that give satisfaction to those who must make the change decisions. With such decisions, there is the risk of failure. Nonetheless, the pressure is there. Knowledge continues to expand. Affluent societies have extended the years of schooling as a solution to the expansion, but how many more years can be added to the educational process without damaging the economic production effort that produces the affluence that makes the added education possible? There is a law governing diminishing returns. Its effect will be to increase the pressure for change in the basic model.

A second force that has contributed to the LCI trend is the development of a workable learning and teaching technology. B.F. Skinner has made major contributions to the field of learning. In his book, *The Technology of Teaching* (1968), he explores how learning theory can be applied to instructional method. Only recently have we begun to impose the requirements of scientific method upon learning theory and educational method (Bigge, 1964). In the process of validation of method, certain techniques have begun to emerge as more effective than others. Skinner (1968) points out that "The advances which have recently been made in our control of the learning process suggest a thorough revision of classroom practices and, fortunately, they tell us how the revision can be brought about." Moreover, as the technology emerges, it lends itself to systematized application to increasingly larger and more complex populations (Silvern, 1972). The technological research that clarified chaining, successive approximation, consequences of behavior, step size, knowledge of results, and active responding allowed the construction of learning methods that were independent of the teacher or trainer. These methods, which include Programmed Instruction and Computer-Assisted Instruction, build the controls *into the learning system* instead of into the teacher. The era may be upon us where we can design learning environments that are more consistently efficient in transmitting knowledge than even the best trainers. This force—the development of a workable teaching technology— directly impacts the feasibility of models, such as LCI, that seek to free the learner and instructor from traditional constraints. The technology allows experimentation. It also demands validation; and validation through scientific method will continue to force the development of alternative models to achieve transfer of knowledge.

A third force leading to the development of LCI has been the emerging emphasis on relevant, measurable learning objectives. Trainers, educators, but most of all learners are demanding that the time spent learning produces useful results. The search for utility has generated a higher level of outcome specification, and this specification has permitted measurement of the learning process. The concern with objectives has led to the prediction of outcomes and has provided us with tools to measure those outcomes. When it became possible to specify outcomes, it also became feasible to delegate learning decisions that deal with the activities of procuring skills and knowledge to the learner.

Objectives, of course, are nothing new. From Plato's *Republic* through today, educational theorists have specu- lated on what the goals of learning should be (Meyer, 1975). Perhaps Huxley (1877) said it best when he noted, "The great end in life is not knowledge but action." Whitehead (1929) devoted a volume to the aims of education and concluded with the position that "Our problem is . . . to fit the world to our perceptions and not our perceptions to the world." In all cases, the focus is on the objective of what is being taught. What is it that we try to accomplish with all this effort? The answer, unfortunately, is sometimes vague. The fog of vagueness begins to burn off the educational landscape when we impose the requirement of measurement upon our objectives. If a thing can be measured, it can be studied. If it can be studied, it can be understood. With understanding comes prediction and control. In Robert Mager's words (1962), "If you're not sure where you're going, you're liable to wind up someplace else—and not even know it." The concept of measurable objectives has aided the development of LCI because the focus is on where one is going and not how one is going to get there. Without a clear vision of the end, discussions about means, such as LCI, become academic.

The fourth factor leading to the development of LCI is the economics of learning. An instructor-controlled, uniformly-paced and sequenced learning experience is, by its very nature, inefficient as a learning vehicle. We know that learners carry their entire reinforcement history with them at all times. We must assume that each person entering a learning environment is different; each person may have a different response to a given stimulus. The same word, the same action may evoke different cues, thus responses, to different people. Because of this, the traditional method of presentation of information through the fixed output of an instructor often fails to evoke appropriate responses. When special effort is made to insure individual comprehension and universal response, it is often at the expense of other learners who sit idly by.

As a presentation device, the instructor does have the advantage of being flexible. Furthermore, some instructors have been known to revise their presentations from time to time, which leads many to believe that they are generally adaptive to the situation. Presentation, though, does not equal learning. When effectiveness is measured by change in learner capability, the instructor is usually found to be less effective and far less consistent than a good program. Effectiveness by itself, however, has never been a prerequisite for change. We have lived with many ineffective methods and procedures in the shadow of those that would produce greater results. It is only when the cost of ineffectiveness becomes intolerable to those who bear that cost that change is mandated. In an affluent environment, inefficiencies are tolerated, but when the affluence begins to fade, results are contrasted with costs.

The last major force influencing the growth of LCI is the increasing availability of low-cost learning resources. Books, magazines, films, filmstrips, tape recordings, slides, games, simulations, closed-circuit television, and even computers are now within the economic limits of most instructional units. With the proliferation of resource materials, it became both possible to utilize all resources and desirable to use the most appropriate. The result is a higher quality and broader variety of resources at the same or lower cost.

The knowledge explosion, the development of the teaching technology, the emphasis on objectives for instruction, the economics of learning, and the increasing availability of resource materials have all contributed to the emergence of Learner Controlled Instruction as a viable instructional design. *It is now possible for us to delegate learning decisions to the learner.*

References

Bigge, M.L. *Learning Theories for Teachers.* New York: Harper and Row, 1964.

Huxley, T.H. *Technical Education,* 1877.

Leonard, G.B. *Education and Ecstasy.* New York: Dell, 1968.

Mager, R.F. *Preparing Instructional Objectives.* Belmont, California: Fearon Publishers, 1962.

Meyer, A.E. *Grandmasters of Educational Thought.* New York: McGraw-Hill, 1975.

Silvern, L.C. *Systems Engineering Applied to Training.* Houston: Gulf, 1972.

Skinner, B.F. *The Technology of Teaching.* New York: Appleton-Century-Crofts, 1968.

United States Department of Health, Education, and Welfare. *Report on Higher Education.* United States Government Printing Office, 1971.

Whitehead, A.N. *The Aims of Education.* (Original edition, 1929.) New York: The Free Press, 1967.

II.

USE

Learner Controlled Instruction is best applied in a resource-rich environment, and our environment—as it concerns knowledge—is becoming richer in resources by the day. Alvin Toffler, in *Future Shock* (1970), points to this when he says, "One can hardly argue that every book is a net gain for the advancement of knowledge. Nevertheless, we find that the accelerative curve of book publication does, in fact, crudely parallel the rate at which man discovered new knowledge." New knowledge is being discovered at an astounding rate. While the volume of printed material being produced is one measure of resources available, it does not capture the magnitude of resource richness that we are beginning to enjoy. In addition to the printed word, we are being bombarded with information resources in all media. Films, slides, programmed texts, filmstrips, computerized instruction, televised information, phonograph records, microfilming, learning games, and tapes—both audio and video—supplement the printed page as information resources.

A resource-rich environment, while necessary, is but one element supporting LCI. Learner Controlled Instruction has been characterized by Langdon (1973) as a grand (or large, overall) strategy or design. Within this strategy, the specific instructional tactics of the designer are applied. The tactics, however, are controlled by both the resources available and the mission. In some cases, LCI is not appropriate. The mission of the designer is often subtly dictated by the environment in which the trained person will be expected to live. If the post-training environment will support individual decision-making, LCI may be an appropriate design. If, on the other hand, the designer knows that the trained learner will be prohibited from making meaningful decisions, LCI should be avoided as an instructional strategy.

From the design aspect, the relationship between mission and method is less important than resource availability. Regardless of all other factors, if a variety of resources is not available on each subject, then the LCI model is not feasible. LCI demands both information resource variety and availability.

Given resources and an appropriate mission, the potential for application of the LCI design can be thought of in the broadest terms. The Infant School movement in England and the Open Classroom trend in the United States are applications of the LCI concept in primary school systems (Featherstone, 1971). We can look to the business sector for more applications of LCI in both basic training and management development (Wydra, 1975). College level courses in psychology have incorporated the LCI design (Sheppard, 1973). Even one-day workshops have been built around the LCI model. The variety of the instructional content in these applications is extensive. The school system applications have included the standard subjects of mathematics, reading, writing, and the sciences. As we move into the business world, the subject matter becomes more diverse. The use of the design, therefore, is not limited by the organizational model or the subject matter. Instead, it is limited by available instructional resources and the mission of the organization.

Since the potential application of the LCI model is broad, it can be utilized for individualized learning programs, independent study programs, or group instruction (if you consider the group as a collection of individuals). Learner Controlled Instruction's most refined application, however, would incorporate all of the aforementioned uses. Imagine an individualized program of independent study administered to a group. Such an application would be possible only when we have large populations of learners and extensive learning resources; nonetheless, it is conceivable. Or, at another extreme, consider the application of the LCI model through a progression of knowledge levels. The learner enters the instructional design as a naive performer, unprepared even to make decisions about what to learn. The learner progresses through levels of knowledge, gaining familiarity, then mastery, and eventually reaching the point where he or she is in a position to enlarge the field of knowledge and to expand the state of the art. If at this point, through categorization of informational resources, the learner could add to the resource availability of the design, he or she would have altered the design while learning from it. The Learner Controlled Instruction design is one of the few instructional vehicles, other than the lecturer, that accommodates constant revision and expansion based upon a changing body of knowledge and available resources.

Considering that the potential application of LCI is so broad, it may be useful to look at some of the constraints that are working upon the designer when this model is used. There are three requirements necessary for the successful use of the LCI design:

1. A variety of content informational *resources* must be available.
2. The designer must be able to state the *objectives* of learning.
3. There must be adequate tools to *measure* the acquisition of a knowledge or skill.

Resources, objectives, measurements—it is around this troika that LCI is built. Content, population, and even the nature of the application are less significant considerations for use of the design. This is because LCI is a grand strategy, a design into which other strategies are placed. There is room in the design for a variety of approaches; therefore, the limitations of some instructional techniques can be countered by an alternate technique. But there is no escaping the need for resources, objectives, and measurements. These are essential.

A moment's reflection will clarify the need for these requirements in the LCI design. In LCI, learners make decisions. In instructor controlled instruction, we can often make judgments and decisions that allow manipulation of the learning outcome based on the responses of the learner. In LCI, we create an environment in which the learner must be capable of making manipulations an instructor would make in a more traditional setting. As designers, we must insure that the learner will have the tools needed for appropriate decisions. To make both manipulations of the learning environment and decisions concerning learning, the learner needs three basic bits of data. The learner needs to know where he or she is going, a means to get there, and a way to know when he or she has arrived.

Knowledge of destination becomes the objective. In a complex course of instruction, there will be many primary sub-objectives. Given learner flexibility, the designer may not—probably will not—know the instructional state of any learner at a given point in time. Therefore, the designer must be able to state all objectives in such a way that the learner can always interpret where he or she is to go or what the outcome of learning is to be.

Since decision involves choice, the learner must have, second, a variety of means, so that choice can occur. And, just as the objectives must be visible to the learner, so must the resources. They provide tangible alternative vehicles that will allow movement toward the objective. In LCI, an objective—no matter how clearly stated or vividly perceived—is not useful unless it can be linked with resources for learning. The objective without learning resources is like man's dream of traveling to Mars without a spaceship. The ends may be there, but not the means.

The third part of the equation, measurement, completes the whole. Measurements allow the learner to gauge a variety of states. Entry knowledge, progress, and mastery are all states of process that require measurement. When measurement of status or progress is left up to an instructor, years of judgment can be used to make accurate assessments. The learner in a LCI mode rarely has the perspective to evaluate his or her status without the use of some prespecified tools.

A learner in LCI must have mechanisms to measure progress. There must be feedback that can be evaluated and qualified by learners. These measurements of status, progress, and mastery must be available to the learner on demand—not at the end of the course. They must be built into the design if they are to aid the learner in assessing accomplishment. They must be built into the design if the learner is to make decisions based on data. And they must be independent of the designer or an instructor. If these are present, the learner can make informed decisions. If they are not, he or she can make educated guesses, which will result in educated mistakes.

LCI is a flexible and creative instructional strategy. Its use is a function of available resources and the nature of the mission of the organization. Given resources and appropriate mission, its major attribute is adaptability to a variety of instructional tactics. Its short-range and long-range applications present an inviting challenge to mature instructional technologists—who have mastered the subtleties of manipulating objectives, resources, and measurements into tools of learning.

References

Featherstone, J. *Schools Where Children Learn.* New York: Avon, 1971.

Langdon, D.G. *Interactive Instructional Designs for Individualized Learning.* Englewood Cliffs, New Jersey: Educational Technology Publications, 1973.

Sheppard, W.C. Presentation on Individualized Learning, National Society for Performance and Instruction Convention, 1973.

Toffler, A. *Future Shock.* New York: Random House, 1970.

Wydra, F.T. Learner Controlled Instruction. *Training Magazine,* August 1975.

III.

OPERATIONAL DESCRIPTION

In the design of a Learner Controlled Instruction program, the objective is to construct an environment that will produce predictable learning results, even though the learner makes many of the learning decisions. Understanding of the learning environment is the key to the successful design of a LCI program. There are stimuli in the environment that will elicit predictable responses from the learner. These must be understood and used by the designer. At the same time, there are consequences in the environment that will reinforce or punish behavior as it is emitted. These too must be understood and used by the designer. There are also learning resources within the environment that must be recognized by the designer if they are to be effectively used. It is the understanding and utilization of these elements within the learning environment that allow the designer to control the outcome of the experience. Therefore, even though the learner controls the *instruction,* the designer controls the *environment.*

To some, it may seem that if the learner is not in absolute control of all elements, then the learner has no control at all. Skinner (1971) addressed this issue when he said:

> It [the literature of freedom] has been forced to brand all control as wrong and to misrepresent many of the

advantages to be gained from a social environment. It is
unprepared for the next step, which is not to free men from
control but to analyze and change the kinds of control to
which they are exposed.

It is our increased understanding of how learning occurs
that allows the delegation of some of the important
instructional decisions. The delegation of these decisions has
the effect of reducing the aversive characteristics of certain
learning tactics as they have impact on the individual. When
the learner has the capability of deciding, then that learner
can avoid situations that are either punishing or non-reinforc-
ing. These situations include, but are not limited to, boredom
caused by redundant instruction or unproductive repetition,
frustration caused by inappropriate presentation levels, and
anxiety resulting from the vagueness of objectives and
performance feedback. An understanding of these situations
forces recognition of the role of the environment in the
learning process. Consequently, as we explore the design of
LCI programs, the primary focus will be on the environment.
It will be considered as a given that, within the framework of
the environment, a variety of learning tactics may be used
and that the learner has control of the major instructional
decisions.

As we begin exploration of the design format for the LCI
environment, it is important to note that the environment is
not a place. Instead, *it is a set of conditions that surround the
learner.* These conditions will include the stimuli that elicit
behaviors as well as the consequences of that behavior. They
include the time frame in which learning takes place as well
as the culture that preconditioned the learner. The physical
place of learning is, of course, important, but it is only one
element in an array of conditions. The design format will
focus on the analysis and organization of those elements in
the environment that will allow the designer to control the

end-result of the program, while delegating the instructional decision.

General LCI Model

The creation of the LCI environment refers to the establishment of an integrated system. Perhaps the best way to look at the LCI concept is to picture it as a system with inputs, processes, outputs, and feedback loops. Figure 1 shows a system that places a naive learner (1.0) into an environment. The output of the processing that takes place in that environment is a trained learner (3.0).

The key features of this model are the learning environment (2.0) and its subsystem—the learning program (2.2). The naive learner entering the learning environment must be provided with a stimulus for learning (2.1). If that stimulus is strong enough, it will propel the learner into the learning program (2.2). If the stimulus in the learning environment is too weak, the learner will not enter the learning program. The solution in this case is, of course, to strengthen the stimulus. Once into the learning program, however, the learner is placed into a variety of learning experiences (2.2.1). The learner progresses through the experiences until the learning program is complete, at which point the learner exits. If the exit is successful, the skills acquired in the total program will be assessed (2.3). When acquired skills are adequate, the learner is passed out of the learning environment and becomes a trained learner (3.0). If, on the other hand, the skills have not been acquired, the learner is looped back through the learning program.

The learning experience (2.2.1) is a subsystem of the learning program subsystem (2.2). However, the learning experience subsystem has a subsystem of its own, as shown in Figure 2.

Within the learning experience subsystem (2.2.1), a stimulus (2.2.1.1) elicits a skill demonstration (2.2.1.2). The

Figure 1

General Model of Learner Controlled Instruction

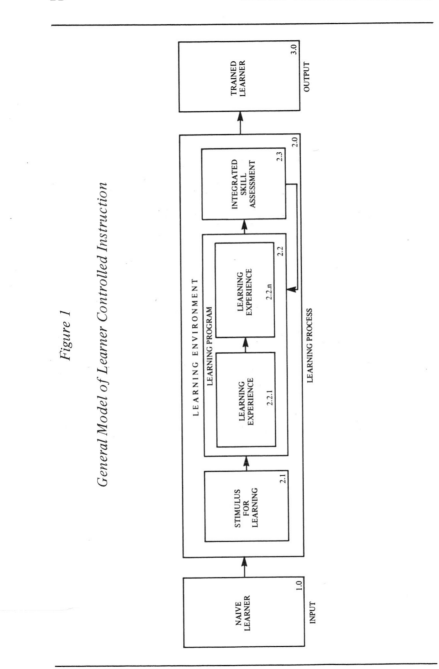

Figure 2

Learning Experience Subsystem

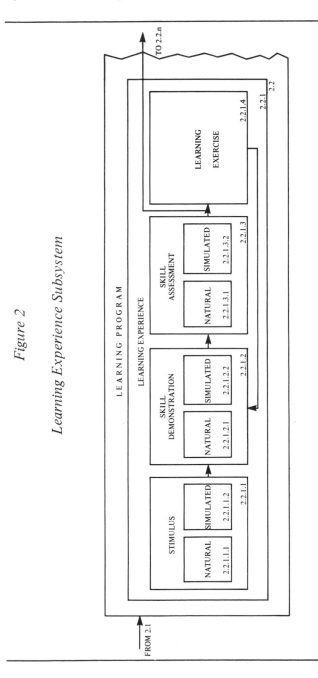

stimulus may be a natural part of the environment (2.2.1.1.1), such as a predictable event, or it may be simulated (2.2.1.1.2). Events that occur in time, such as nightfall, a change of seasons, or the beginning of the week, are examples of natural stimuli. Examples of other types of natural stimuli are predictable confrontations, such as a disagreement, or predictable problems, such as recurring job vacancies. The key points in utilizing natural stimuli (2.2.1.1.1) are that they have a high probability of occurring at an appropriate time and that they are relevant to the learning objective. When these conditions exist, they can be used to trigger a skill demonstration. However, we are not always lucky enough to have the right stimuli occur at the right time. Then, we, as designers, have to create an engineered or simulated stimulus (2.2.1.1.2) to elicit the desired skill demonstration. Probably the simplest way to produce action is to give a command, such as, "complete the cash accounting forms." More complex simulated stimuli will involve the creation of situations that appear to be natural, such as the sounding of a fire alarm or a role-play telephone call.

The entire purpose of the stimulus is to produce the skill demonstration (see Figure 3). The demonstration is a set of behaviors that will—after measurement against a standard—determine whether or not learning is required. In conventional instructional designs, little if any credit is given for previously learned skills. Learner Controlled Instruction, through skill demonstration, provides an opportunity for the learner to by-pass the learning exercise, thus avoiding the redundancy of being exposed to exercises designed to teach already learned skills.

Non-productive learning exercises—those that deal with skills already acquired—are major drags on the efficiency of most learning systems. The skill demonstration (2.2.1.2), like other subsystems in the learning experience subsystem, may

Figure 3

Skill Demonstration Subsystem

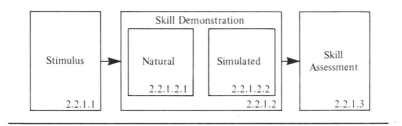

be natural (2.2.1.2.1) or simulated (2.2.1.2.2). Natural demonstrations (2.2.1.2.1) are those where the learner actually demonstrates the skill under conditions that are inherent in the environment. Taking a driving test on a street or road is one such example. Operating a computerized automobile could be considered an effective substitute for the open-road test, but it is a simulated (2.2.1.2.2), not real, demonstration.

As a rule of thumb, demonstrations under natural conditions are superior to simulated conditions. They produce the most realistic behavior on the part of the learner. Unfortunately, natural conditions also create the most difficult circumstances in which to measure the behavior. For example, the most realistic measure of whether a learner can land an aircraft is to turn the controls over to him or her in mid-flight. The demonstration will conclusively prove the presence or absence of the skill, but the risk of possible damage to the plane, learner, and evaluator is high. In addition, measurements of skill demonstration under natural conditions are sometimes not discriminating enough to be useful in analysis of learning deficiencies; that, of course, is the purpose of the skill demonstration at this stage. When risk or the potential for damage is low, or when the results will be unambiguous, the skill demonstration under natural conditions is preferable to simulation. In those instances where simulation is used, care should be taken to duplicate natural conditions as completely as possible. Only the elements of risk and ambiguity should be removed.

The skill demonstration subsystem (2.2.1.2) feeds the skill assessment subsystem (2.2.1.3), as illustrated in Figure 4. Skill assessment allows measurements by the learner as to whether or not the competency is present.

In LCI, the learner is a key decision-maker. The decision in assessment is one of competency. It is to be made by the learner and will determine future action. If the demonstration is assessed as adequate, the learner will exit that learning experience and will move to the next experience (2.2.n). Demonstrations assessed as less than competent will, on the other hand, lead to a learning exercise (2.2.1.4). The process is familiar to all who evaluate learning; only the decision-maker is different.

The key difficulty in the skill assessment subsystem is that the naive learner doesn't know what he or she doesn't know. The experience base used by master performers in making competency decisions is missing. If a master performer were on the scene to assess the performance, he or she could draw on his or her experience and decide if the demonstration exhibited competency, but in the LCI scheme of things, the master performer will seldom—if ever—be on the scene.

To counter this difficulty, the designer must create or identify conditions in the environment that will enable the naive learner to assess his or her own competency. Easier said than done!

Assessment involves two elements: a measuring tool and a standard. These terms are often treated as interchangeable, but they are not the same. A ruler is a measurement tool; it identifies differences in distance. A jury is a measurement tool; it identifies the facts of a matter. Neither ruler nor jury

Figure 4

Skill Assessment Subsystem

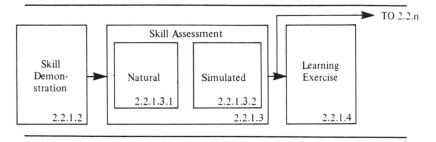

is a standard. A standard is a mechanism that allows interpretation of differences. The jury interprets facts against the standard of the law. The standard of the marksman is whether he or she can hit the bull's-eye, but the target is the measurement tool. The graduated rings of the target identify differences in the accuracy of the shot. Without a target, there would not be a measurement tool. Without the measurement, there cannot be a standard, and the standard is generally a function of the measurement tool.

To make an assessment of competency, the learner needs three things:

(1) a measurement tool;

(2) a process for using the measurement tool; and

(3) a standard.

As with stimuli and demonstrations, the elements of assessment are often found in the environment. If the skill demonstration is completion of standard accounting forms, a natural measurement, or one contained in the environment, might be either the cross-balance process or auditors. As LCI designers, we can take advantage of these non-contrived or natural measurements to aid the learner in assessment of the adequacy of the demonstration. Carrying this example a bit further, the learner would need to know that cross-balancing and/or regular audits are part of the measurement process. The knowledge that one balance must be checked against another or the inspection by auditors is knowledge of the process of the measurement discipline. If the process were not in place, it would need to be invented. Finally, the learner needs to know the standard. How many errors are acceptable? One? Ten percent of the entries? Three arithmetic and no procedural? The definition of the standard is also frequently defined by the environment. In the example we are using, the standard might be that the accounting forms balance or that they are approved as correct by the auditor. These standards are already contained in the environment. They can be considered part of the natural assessment (2.2.1.3.1).

Once again, if the elements of assessment are not naturally present in the environment, they must be contrived by the designer. If the accounting forms used in this skill demonstration do not require balancing, or if no auditor regularly inspects them, then the designer must contrive or simulate the mechanism for assessment. The measurement tool in this case might be a correctly filled out form used for reference. The mechanism for use could be a simple comparison, and the standard could be a predefined number of errors. The tool, its use, and the standard are all simulated; they are not naturally found in the environment. However, this simulated assessment (2.2.1.3.2) aids the learner in determining the adequacy of the skill demonstration.

Whether natural or simulated, the learner needs a vehicle to assess the adequacy of the skill demonstration. In LCI, the designer must know the environment well enough to determine if mechanisms for assessment exist. If not, he or she must design them and place them at the learner's disposal. This is an integral part of the model.

At this point in the model, the only thing the learner has learned is whether or not learning is needed. That, in itself, is a great deal, but for our purposes it is not enough. The learner must now be routed to another assessment of his or her skills or, if necessary, to some vehicle that will provide for a transfer of skills or knowledge.

Figure 5 shows that in exiting the skill assessment module (2.2.1.3), the learner may follow one of two paths. If the assessment shows competency, the learner exits the subsystem. After exit, the learner may go to either another learning experience (2.2.n), or, if all experiences have been completed, to the integrated skill assessment (2.3) of the learning environment (2.0). However, if the skill of the learner is less than adequate, he or she moves into a learning exercise (2.2.1.4).

Learning exercises are those activities that allow the learner to gain competency in a skill. In most instructional settings, it is this module that is considered the "program." In LCI, it is usually an array of programs or structured activities. The common denominator of the programs is that they will provide the learner with a method of gaining competency.

The learning exercise is the event in which the learners, using the resources provided, will train themselves. Since only naive learners—those who failed to show competency on the skill demonstration as measured by the assessment—entered the learning exercise, we still need to verify their competency. Consequently, the only exit from the learning exercise (2.2.1.4) is to the skill demonstration (2.2.1.2). This is the designer's feedback loop. This is the loop to analyze in determining whether or not the learning experience is working. Given a skill demonstration and assessment powerful enough to discriminate between competent and incompetent performers, the test of the learning exercise is the number of demonstrations required before the learner exits from the experience. If either the objective or resources are faulty, the learner is trapped. He or she will never legitimate-

Figure 5

Learning Experience Subsystem

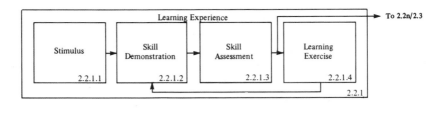

ly exit the experience. If they are effective, most previously naive learners will exit on the first pass.

As shown in Figure 6, learners who exit the learning experience (2.2.1) move on to the next learning experience (2.2.2) and then to the next, *ad infinitum* (2.2.n), until they have mastered all required skills in the learning program (2.2). They then exit the learning program (2.2) and enter the integrated skill assessment (2.3).

It is in this module that the learner skills are tested as a whole. It is here that the permutations and combinations of random real-life performance, integrating all relevant skills, are elicited and assessed. Often, skills are adequately mastered in isolation, but when their use is integrated with other learned skills, failure occurs. At other times, the interfaces between skills have not been adequately mastered. The integrated skill assessment addresses and tests these potential deficiencies. The assessment in this module duplicates the learning experience assessment, but on a grander scale. It insures that the whole of performance is at least equal to the sum of its parts. If the performance is not up to standard, the learner is routed back into the learning program (2.2) to develop integration skills. On the other hand, if performance

Figure 6

Learning Environment Subsystem

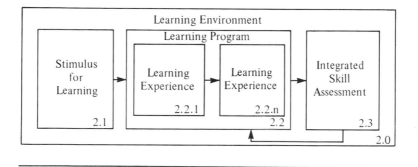

is adequate, the learner exits the module and the learning environment (2.0) to become a trained learner (3.0).

Summary

In summary, the LCI general model experience places a naive learner in a learning environment and outputs a trained learner. The learning environment contains a stimulus for learning, a learning program, and a vehicle for assessing integrated skill acquirements. The core process element is the learning program, which is composed of a variety of learning experiences, each providing for some natural or simulated stimulus, skill demonstration, and skill assessment. There are also learning exercises for learners who cannot initially demonstrate competency. Learners demonstrating skills that meet the standard, as measured by the designated tool, pass out of the learning experience and into either another learning exercise or to the integrated skill assessment module of the learning environment. The movement through the system is largely controlled by the learner. It is the designer, however, who has the responsibility for the construction of the entire system and all of its elements. The designer's task is to create the environment in which the learner can control his or her own learning.

Reference

Skinner, B.F. *Beyond Freedom and Dignity.* New York: Alfred A. Knopf, 1971.

IV.

DESIGN FORMAT

Learner Controlled Instruction is first and foremost an instructional strategy. As such, it should not be limited by form. Its nature is one of flexibility. Often, the artifacts of a learning design or model limit the thinking of the designer. In LCI, while some discussion of format may be useful as an aid to understanding concepts, it must be recognized that it is the *concept,* not the format or artifact, that governs.

In Learner Controlled Instruction, there are two separate and distinct format focal points. The first is the Format of the Learning Experience. The other is the Format of the Overall Design. Each has its own requirements. In the following sections, these requirements will be examined and illustrated.

I. Format of the Learning Experience
Format, as it is used here, is how the elements of the program are arranged for presentation to and for use by the learner. In LCI, as in life, the learner often does not know what he or she does not know. Our task in formatting, then, is to provide the learner with efficient, effective mechanisms with which to access elements of the program. This is quite different from the presentation mode. The skill of navigating the learning experience is important. But here the skill is not the objective. Instead, it is the package and process that allow the skill to be practiced.

33

The learner entering the environment the designer has created will need a road map to find his or her way around. In a learning program there will be, in all probability, a multitude of learning experiences. To aid in the movement among these experiences, a common, standardized format will facilitate understanding. A side-benefit of standardization will be a reduction of learning time. If the format of the learning experiences is standardized, the learner will not need to master a new set of access rules for each experience.

In each learning experience, the designer provides the learner with information about objectives, evaluations, and resources. The learner needs to know the what, when, where, and how of each of these. A matrix (see Figure 7) can be constructed that highlights the key questions that need to be addressed in the format. Each cell in the matrix provides a test for the format.

The instructions to the learner can be communicated visually or by means of audio. The visual presentation may be verbal or graphic, and it may be electronic, mechanical, or the plain old printed word. Regardless of the mechanism for presentation, the instructions must be presented if the learner is to move through the experience. The organization of these instructions into a standard pattern creates the format.

A visual, verbal, printed format is the most expedient. This is often the least expensive, most easily revised map that can be placed in the hands of a learner. The learner can access it without any special devices and can refer forward or backward in sequence as suits his or her fancy. Sometimes, printed pages in loose leaf books and at other times index cards are used, but they always contain certain elements:

(1) a description of the activity to be performed;
(2) the measurements and standards used in evaluation; and
(3) the resources available to the learner.

The language used to communicate the instructions is kept

Figure 7

Key Concerns in Format

	WHAT	WHEN	WHERE	HOW
OBJECTIVE	What is it?	Is there a special time?	Is there a special place?	Are there constraints?
EVALUATION	What is to be evaluated?	Time?	Place?	What measurements & standards are to be used?
RESOURCE	Are they available?	Any time constraints?	Any location constraints?	Are special instructions needed for use?

simple for clarity. All of the pertinent information identified in the matrix in Figure 7 is covered in one section or another. For example, using a task of planning a sale and then selling the product, the form shown in Figure 8 illustrates how each of the points of the matrix is addressed.

The sequencing of the information on the page is not important, as long as it is consistent. The sequence in the previous example has been selected because it follows a natural progression. The learner is informed about what is to be done, how to measure its accomplishment, and if needed, the resources to pursue if performance is below standard.

Once past the format of the learning experience instructions, the task of categorizing and describing the resources must be addressed so that the learner can more easily and efficiently access the subject matter. Learners should be able to retrieve as much subject matter as is necessary for the accomplishment of the objectives. As mentioned earlier, one of the major hazards in LCI is that learners don't know what they don't know. Nor do they know how much they need to know. The learner may wish to go into the subject matter in extreme detail; he or she may wish to review the subject matter; he or she may wish to do reference work utilizing the subject matter; or he or she may wish to simply browse. To execute his or her wishes, the learner can be provided a guide of the subject matter keyed to the objectives. For instructional travelers, the guides, or maps, serve the same purpose that road maps do for geographical travelers.

By formatting both the instructions to the learners (learning maps) and the resource materials (information maps), learners are provided with a route that will quickly and easily move them through the exercise. These mechanisms make it easier for learners to see where it is they are going. Consequently, they can get there with a minimum of false starts.

Information maps, discussed at length by Horn *et al.* (1971), are used to organize the access to resource or learning

Figure 8

Diagram of Employee Induction Activity

REQUIRED ACTIVITY #51: Sales Planning and Merchandising—In-store Promotion

ACTIVITY DESCRIPTION:

The objective tells what is to be done, to whom, when it is to be done, and where.

Select one profitable item each from the Grocery, Meat and Produce departments that you decide is worthy of a one-week promotional effort. These items must be sold at the published retail price and not advertised. Take whatever steps necessary to set up your own Sales Promotion for these items. Design your program to include displaying, signing, location and any other action needed to make your promotion successful.

Document this Activity on Worksheet SP-4 (one for each item in each department).

MEASUREMENT AND STANDARDS:

The evaluation identifies the measurements and standards to be used as well as the time and place of evaluation.

At completion of Activity:

Meeting or exceeding Sales and Profit objective .... Excellent
Within 25% of Sales and Profit objective... Satisfactory
Under 25% of Sales and Profit objective .... Unsatisfactory (Repeat)

RESOURCES:

The Resources show special constraints and instructions.

Documents—
All District, Division policies and procedures related to In-Store Promotions
Past Weekly Sales Plans

NOTE: All documents were provided to learner at beginning of program.

People—
Store Manager
Store Department Heads
Specialists
District Manager

TIME PLAN:	Projected	Actual
Beginning Date:	....	....
Completion Date:	....	....

Reference Time for Trained Employee: 4 hours total.

NOTES:

materials. Since their objective is to facilitate access to content, they allow movement through materials to meet the learners' needs. Information maps could be characterized as indexes that change standard resources into branched programs.

Information maps, though elegant in concept, require discipline in application. To truly aid the learner, the map-maker must be consistent in use, placement, and definition of words and symbols. But, that discipline provides benefits beyond those experienced by the learner. Once mapped, the materials can be mechanically or electronically stored, manipulated, and retrieved. They can be made available to large populations at low cost. They can be revised in whole or part as the situation demands. The discipline of information mapping provides resource utilization flexibility to both the learner and the designer.

Learning maps differ from information maps. Learning maps assume defined objectives and then detail alternate routes. Though information maps allow easy movement through resources, they assume neither objective nor route.

Accomplishment is often measured by degree. The same objective may have differing levels of accomplishment. Learning maps are useful in guiding learner movement to the appropriate level as well as route. For example, in a LCI workshop on LCI, the primary subject matter was divided into ten interest areas. Each interest area, such as learning maps, utilization of resources, establishment of objectives, etc., was further subdivided into at least three levels of accomplishment. Higher levels of accomplishment required responses that were progressively more sophisticated. Each interest area and level also had multiple learning resources available. A learner entering the workshop was faced with a potentially bewildering array of options. However, learners were provided with maps that showed the relationships between objectives, levels of accomplishment, and resources.

As a result, most learners easily and quickly navigated the instructional landscape and reached the learning objective.

Though they serve different purposes, both information and learning maps aid the designer in establishing the format and sequence of the program. They provide organization to resources and sequence while preserving learner choice.

II. Format of the Overall Design

Just as each learning experience and resource needs formatting, so does the overall program. Imagine a naive learner given a set of individual learning experience instructions, say 90 or 100 pages, and perhaps 150 to 200 assorted books, pamphlets, tapes, etc. Without some format to the overall design, without some general organization and instruction, the learner will be hopelessly bewildered. To avoid that situation, at least six kinds of information need to be given to the learner:

(1) a general introduction to the program, including a statement as to objectives and concepts;

(2) instructions as to how to proceed through the program;

(3) a description of the types of materials that will be encountered;

(4) an introduction to special situations, people, resources, or equipment;

(5) an overview as to schedule and sequence; and

(6) a mechanism to solicit help when progress is blocked or trouble occurs.

Other items can be provided, based upon the complexity or design of the program. The choice is the designer's, but the ultimate goal is to provide the learner with advance information concerning the learning experience.

1. General Introduction

The general introduction may be a letter or audiotape to

the learner, but it should clearly say, "START HERE" or "PRESS THIS BUTTON FIRST." It should explain what is to be accomplished. The learner controlled model of instruction will be foreign to many learners. To help them gain familiarity, describe the overall concept of the program. Tell them the decisions they are expected to make and those that will be made by others. Tell about the constraints and the freedoms of both the program and the environment. The more information given to learners at this point, the better they will be able to handle the tasks that lay ahead.

2. How to Proceed Through the Program

The learner also needs to know how his or her movement through the program will be monitored. The following is an excerpt from one LCI program introduction to the trainee (Wydra, 1968):

> Your projects have been arranged in a sequence which will lead to rapid learning. Most of the time you will be working on several activities at the same time. Some activities only require an hour or so of your time each day for several weeks. Others can be totally completed in a day or two. Your judgment will determine which activities you should be working on at any given time.

In addition, the learner must understand the theory of the program. Confidence in his or her ability has already been demonstrated by the very nature of the efforts that went into designing the program. Reaffirm that confidence once again by assuming that he or she will understand your theory. Otherwise, the risk is that the learner will attempt to interpret this program consistent with his or her past experiences. Such actions will insure a high probability of failure and/or frustration, neither of which is useful in a successful learning experience. To avoid this, explain the theory in the introduction. A map to guide the learners into and through the program—to aid them in getting started—is also helpful.

3. Types of Materials

A third essential item is a description of the types of learning materials that will be used as resources.

Great detail is not necessary, but it is useful to the learner to know that the subject matter may be presented in a variety of ways. Some learners have an aversion to specific types of presentation modes. Their preconceptions about presentation modes sometimes inhibit their entry into the program. In addition, it is likely that the learners will have at their disposal more material than those with which they will interact. Traditional learning experiences often involve "going through the materials." The thought of "going through" a visible resource bank may discourage the most dedicated learner. The learners can overcome these apprehensions if they know the types of materials to which they will be exposed. They also need to know that because of the instructional model, there will be a duplication of subject matter. They should have the sense that they are the proverbial kids in the resource candy store. They can pick favorites as a steady treat while experimenting with the more exotic (for them) presentation modes.

4. Special Situations

Typically, resources will be available at a single location. That location may be a place or a package. In one LCI setting, all learners go to a resource center where the materials are available. This is economical with large groups of learners who are in geographical proximity of each other. Another setting might involve packaging all resources in a box and sending them to learners. While this may seem extravagant, it is economical when the cost of resources is less than the cost of temporarily relocating the learner. In either case, most resources with which the learner will interact are centralized, whether the location be a room or a box. There are, however, resources that cannot be made continually available to the learner. People, conditional situations, expensive equipment, and facilities fall into this category. Often, these resources add depth and dimension to the learning exercise. The learner should be told about these resources as he or she is introduced to the program. Knowledge of these special resources will also assure the learner that there will be opportunity for non-programmed contact and feedback. The introduction may be as unobtrusive as a listing of who, what, and when the learner will encounter, or it may involve individualized, personalized introductions explaining role and function. At either extreme, the learner will benefit from the advance information by allowing insights into the experience that will aid in scheduling and sequencing.

5. Overview of Schedule

The fifth item provided to the learner is the overview of schedule and sequence. By now, the learner knows where he or she is going but needs some information on how he or she is going to get there and how long it will take. A device that is useful in accomplishing this task is the activity/time matrix. The matrix lists the major projects, tasks, activities, etc., in an overall rough sequence along one axis. Those accomplishments that are prerequisites for later activities are sequenced in a position that will allow their completion prior to the start of activities that are dependent upon them. Generalization activities that flow from an initial learning experience are sequenced accordingly. The other axis of the matrix gives a guide to the time relationships for each activity and between them. For example, in a course for middle managers in industry, the Activity/Time Matrix shown in Figure 9 was used.

Figure 9

Sample Activity/Time Matrix

	ACTIVITY		PROGRAM TIME IN WEEKS				
No.	Description	1	2	3	4	5	6
1.	Orientation/Introduction	X					
2.	Orientation to Labor Laws	X					
3.	Orientation to Accounting Principles	X	X				
4.	Orientation to Supervisory Practices	X					
5.	Labor Contracts Interpretation			X	X		
6.	Time Reporting			X			
7.	Work Scheduling				X	X	
8.	Accounting Policies					X	X

As Figure 9 illustrates, the orientation or overview activities precede the more sophisticated activities of interpreting labor contracts or applying interpretations to a work schedule. The time of application for some activities is short, while others may require extended time. The performance criteria, in most cases, dictate the minimum time required to demonstrate competence. The maximum time will, of course, be a function of the individual learner's learning history. However, the demographic analysis, which will be explored in the Developmental Guide chapter, acts as a valuable aid in making generalizations about prior experience, and thus learning times, for the population as a whole.

In providing the overview to schedule and sequence, a note of caution from the designer to the learner is in order. The designer's overview is at best a general approximation of the path and time that will apply to any individual learner. Certainly, the farther removed the learner is from the first activity, the less he or she will be able to draw on the designer's generalization. Sequence and schedule will become a function of his or her experiences in the program and not of the designer's plan. He or she needs to know that. Emphasize that all we can do is provide a general framework to give an overview of the task. His or her actual pattern will be dictated by his or her experiences. The learner must be cautioned not to attempt to meet the sequence/schedule framework that has been established. To do so will waste time on those things at which he or she has already become proficient and hurry those activities that may require more learning time.

6. How to Seek Help

Finally, the trainee needs to be informed about mechanisms that will assist him or her when progress is blocked or trouble occurs. In most LCI programs, the designer will not be available. Your best option is to assign some person—an instructor, facilitator, coordinator, or whatever title you and your organization fancy—to aid the trainee when trouble occurs, and it *will*: "The tape recorder doesn't work." "You left out the text on psychocybernetics." "My jelly sandwich slipped out of my hand and landed on the videotape." Invent your own potential problems, but your learners will find situations that will make your imagination look dull. So, anticipate problems by requiring that some warm, knowledgeable, and accessible human being be available when help is needed.

Other Documents Needed

These, then, will be the designer's major considerations as preliminary design is placed into a format. The focus is on the learner and the tools needed to move through the program. The preliminary design will, generally, be summarized in one or two documents: The "Administrative Manual" and the "Instructions to the Learner(s) Manual." It is most useful to prepare both of these documents immediately after the learning experiences have been completed.

The "Administrative Manual," addressed to the people who will manage the program, focuses on those guidelines that deal with establishing the environment, selecting learners, arranging resources, introducing the learners to the program, etc. It deals with things that surround the learning experience. The "Instructions to the Learner(s) Manual," on the other hand, addresses situations the learner will need to handle. Objective, scope, method, decision-making, etc., are part of this document. Between them they will detail most of the six items noted above.

References

Horn, R. *et al. A Reference Collection of Rules and Guidelines for Writing Information Mapped Materials.* Lexington, Massachusetts: Information Resources, Inc., 1971.

Wydra, F.T. Store Management Training Program, in use at Allied Supermarkets, Inc., Detroit, 1968.

V.

OUTCOMES

Why should the Learner Controlled Instruction model be used? What will it produce that other models do not? Is the investment worth the price? Valid questions. They can be best answered by looking at the outcomes of applying the model to a learner situation.

The LCI model allows the learner to make decisions about the learning process he or she is using. The model does not, however, delegate decisions about learning objectives, measurements, or standards. These are all specified by the designer, even though the learner has an opportunity to use them. The assumption, then, is that the manipulation of the learning process by the learner is more efficient than the same manipulation by the instructor. If the assumption is true, we should be able to measure it by looking at the effect on learning acquisition of knowledge and at the cost of that acquisition to the individual and society.

Learner acquisition of knowledge is the first test of any instructional model. If the learner fails to learn, the model is useless, regardless of its popularity. One of the precepts of LCI is that its transfer of knowledge capability must be validated. We can, therefore, dispense with the first test. If the design is not validated as a transfer mechanism, it is not LCI. It may be learner controlled "something else," but it is not Learner Controlled Instruction.

A second test of an instructional model is its effectiveness when compared to other models. We know that learning can occur. We have thousands of years of results to prove that point. Effectiveness, though, measures the relative degrees of success one process has over another. For example, in training pigeons, LCI would be less effective than other models. Pigeons have not yet acquired the higher-level skills that allow them to access various available resources. In fairness to pigeons, there are also situations in which LCI is not an appropriate vehicle for training higher-level beings. These situations are those where:

(1) the objectives are so fluid that they cannot be unambiguously specified (i.e., many college courses);

(2) the resources for information are limited or structured so as to provide no choice for the learner;

(3) the measurement tools have not been refined to the point where they can be used by a non-expert;

(4) the time does not exist to conduct an adequate analysis regarding the environment and its consequences;

(5) the instructional content is so limited as to not be worth the effort to develop an elaborate program; and

(6) the population is so small that the cost of developing a program is greater than its benefits.

These common conditions rule out utilization of LCI in a good number of situations. However, the remaining situations in which LCI can be applied are still numerous. When objectives, resources, measurements, time, content, and population are present, LCI becomes competitive on an effectiveness basis with instructor controlled instructional models. It is cheaper, more flexible, and less aversive to both learner and instructor, and it may reduce acquisition time.

I. The Economics of LCI

The economics of LCI begin with the presence of large populations and varied subject matter. There are four economic considerations that it is useful to review. These are the cost of facilities, instructors, resources, and learner time. A closer look at each of these factors will provide evidence of the concrete, beneficial outcomes of LCI versus other instructional forms.

Facilities. Until now, our instructional facilities have been designed to house people instead of to accommodate transfer of knowledge. As things go, people are relatively large—larger than a sixty minute cassette tape for instance—and, therefore, require large amounts of space. LCI begins to allow us to make maximum use of the existing non-academic environment for learning. The existing homes, places of work, entertainment spas, and so forth, become the environment of learning. The special facilities designed to monitor people "doing their learning assignments" or receiving instruction are eliminated. In one LCI program, hundreds of people were trained in a variety of skills to fairly exacting standards and they never once entered a classroom. The facility cost to process these learners through a classroom environment would have been several hundred thousand dollars versus the several thousands that were actually spent. As LCI programs are developed, facilities to house resources and perhaps instruction on a learner demand basis will be needed. But we will certainly not need continual shelter for the entire learner population. The environment already contains that shelter. Let's use it!

The Instructor. The second economic factor is the instructor. Instructors cost money. In these roles, they are far less reliable and consistent than other devices, such as computers and videotapes. They are, after all, human. On an economic basis, however, they have developed a habit that makes them relatively expensive; they like to get paid on a regular basis.

Since salaries of instructors are the greatest visible cost of traditional instruction, any devices which increase their efficiency should reduce cost. However, using conventional instructor controlled instruction, the efficiency of an instructor is limited by a statistic called size. True, in some lecture situations, instructors have managed to stretch class size into the hundreds, but then they often have a number of assistants to help them handle the administrative duties. By the time the assistants finish clarifying the lecture, they too have become bound by class size. The problem here may well be that the instructor is asked to perform in too many roles. Course designer, presenter, feedback agent, auditor, evaluator, controller, and administrator are some of the more significant roles of instructors. This set of roles has not substantially changed since Socrates. In 1776, Adam Smith in his *Wealth of Nations* articulated the economic advantages of divisions of labor. With such a division, each process can be developed to its maximum. One of the characteristics of LCI is that it allows specialization. It also allows mechanization of routine tasks and delegation of decision-making to less highly trained individuals. With these advantages, the person who filled the role of instructional generalist can become one of a smaller army of instructional specialists. The net effect of specialization, delegation, and mechanization should be to produce a lower per student cost.

As we move toward a world more and more influenced by computer technology, the effect of decentralization of the learning experience, from instructor controlled and classroom bound to learner controlled and classroomless, will become more pronounced. Even today, micro-computers are invading home and work place. The cost of these computers was down to under $500.00 in 1979. As this trend progresses, there will be increased demand for software to accommodate LCI and self-instructional modes. The satisfaction of that demand will forever alter the role of instructors.

The emphasis will be on using the human brain to create and not to regurgitate. The per unit cost of course development may increase. The cost of presentation should decrease.

Resources. A third economic factor is the cost of artifacts to be used as learning resources. They are, at the same time, becoming more and less costly. For less than an hour's work at the minimum wage rate, anyone can acquire copies of man's greatest writing. They may be bound in paper and printed with ink that smudges. But, they are available at low cost. Inexpensive magazines and journals chronicle theories and proofs of intellectual achievement. The Instamatic, Polaroid, and 35mm slide cameras give us visual representation of reality for pennies. The audio-cassette captures sound that in the past could only be described by inadequate words. These low-cost resources allow low-cost transfer of information. They also allow freedom of choice by the learner. Through that choice, the learner can match learning resource with learning style. The resources make choice, flexibility, and the resulting efficiency possible.

Learner Time. The efficiency in use of resources is a key element leading to the fourth economic advantage of LCI, learner time. In addition to being a segment of the population categorized as "learners," learners have other roles. The most critical of these is that they are also producers. They are the human resource of our society. To be producers, however, they must be producing and not learning.

Learning is an activity that expends resources, while production increases them. Learning is often a good investment. The resources invested multiply because of the applied knowledge of the learner. But time spent learning is a consumptive rather than a productive activity.

If learning time can be reduced, the learner has the opportunity to either start producing or to use the time to acquire more knowledge. The assumption in either case is that the knowledge will some day be put to use. Reduced learning times, therefore, will lead to higher levels of production because of either longer production times or more effective use of investment capital in the form of subject matter mastered. Industry is aware of this fact as evidenced by its insistence on short learning times. The academic world is only now becoming aware of this concept. More content is being introduced in a set time frame, and speedier matriculation is being encouraged. Both have the effect of strengthening the productive capability of the human resource.

LCI takes advantage of the situation because it capitalizes on the prior experience of a learner. It uses past knowledge as a base and lets the learner decide where to start the instructional process. This eliminates redundant "teaching" and thus reduces learning time. Further, the LCI model allows individualization of learning resources and patterns. These characteristics of the model allow the learner to navigate the content maze in the shortest possible time frames.

II. The Transfer of Power in LCI

While LCI has considerable economic charm, it has an even more significant force supporting it, a useful realignment of power.

Learner Controlled Instruction is a teaching strategy that can accommodate instructional techniques such as self-instruction, criterion-referenced instruction, proficiency examinations, and consequence management. It can accommodate any variety of presentation devices, whether they be conventional or innovative, but its essence is not its ability to accommodate a technique. Instead, the essence of LCI is its transfer of power.

In conventional learning models, the learner knows what he or she knows. His or her experiences through life have provided him or her with a knowledge base. The instructor, on the other hand, knows the object of the training and has some concept of key relationships in the content of information that will facilitate the transfer of knowledge. However, the instructor does not know, on an individual basis, just what it is that the learner already knows. The result of this situation is that both the learner and the instructor have key bits of information, but neither really knows the answer to the critical question—what is it that the learner doesn't know? The learner knows what he or she knows but doesn't know what he or she doesn't know. The instructor knows what he or she would like to have known but doesn't know what the learner knows; and, therefore, cannot complete the equation of subtracting the known from the sum to identify the missing amount. With the instructor in the position of power to make decisions, the only alternative is for the instructor to assume or guess at the information that is known by the learner. Most of the time, these are accurate assumptions and guesses, but often they are not. When the assumption of present learner knowledge is wrong, the effect is either a bored or befuddled learner. To overcome the effect of the assumption error, we have required the presence of an instructor at the learning site. The instructor, by evaluating responses of the learner, adjusts the assumption of what is known by the learner and, consequently, of what must be learned. This technique, however, is better adapted to handling befuddlement than boredom. The consequences are that too many learners no longer find the learning environment, including the instructor, stimulating. Without the stimulus, the learner doesn't respond. Without the response, the opportunity for the instructor to reinforce is reduced and may eventually be extinguished. All this occurs because the person making the decision of what is to be learned lacks a critical piece of information—what is not known.

The learner, though, is in no better a position. Not knowing what he or she doesn't know, he or she has no reference points that can help him or her bridge the gap from ignorance to knowledge. The strategy of LCI attempts to overcome that deficiency. At the same time, it transfers the power of deciding the quantity of the knowledge gap from the instructor to the learner. That transfer is the key. It shifts responsibility for decision-making to the learner and thus allows the use of all previous learning as a reference point. Using previous learning, informed decisions about pace, sequence, content, and mastery can be made.

The learner is in a better position to complete the equation than is the instructor. The knowledge of what it is he or she knows is both vaporous and individual. He or she, therefore, is in a better position to make valid assumptions about it. It is his or her knowledge that is being assumed. For the learner it is not an assumption; it is a known. It is only an assumption for the instructor. If, then, we provide the learner with a second known quantity, namely a description of the objective of learning, then the learner and only the learner has two of the three parts of the equation. He or she is, therefore, in a far better, more informed, position to make decisions than is the instructor. It is this situation that produces the outcomes of Learner Controlled Instruction. It is this situation that allows the transfer of decision-making, the power to decide, from the instructor to the learner. If we assume that, along with subject matter content and instructional process, the instructor is also transferring a set of values, then we can begin to understand the force that is being delegated to the learner. The value system of the learner will become the function of data and not of the presenter, and that indeed is a transfer of a significant power. To allow such a transfer as a function of an instructional design is an elegantly simple way of divorcing learners from the prejudices of the teachers.

VI.

THE DEVELOPMENTAL GUIDE

The general model explored in the Operational Description chapter provides us with a conceptual framework within which a LCI program can be constructed. It acts as a guide to strategy decisions, but the actual construction of the program is often more of an exercise in tactics than strategy. As a guide to tactics, it may be helpful to explore a procedure that has been useful in constructing LCI programs.

Learner Controlled Instruction programs, like many other instructional efforts, can justifiably be compared to icebergs; the visible area contains only a small portion of the mass. The bulk of the program is represented by the research and analytical and design work that precedes production. The visible end result of the LCI design effort will be a set of learning exercises formulated into a program, but the foundation upon which these artifacts are built is the integrity of the design effort.

There are seven major steps in the Learner Controlled Instruction design process:

    I. Define the mission.
    II. Define the population.
    III. Define the required performance results.
    IV. Define the environmental specifications.
    V. Construct the learning experience.
    VI. Validate the design.
    VII. Package the program.

Each step relates to one or more of the systems or modules in the general model. As the procedure is developed, it will be related to the general model for clarity. As an overview, though, let's look at how the entire design procedure interacts with the general model.

Figure 10 shows that the first step of the design process, defining the mission, involves the entire model. Step II, defining the population, establishes the input requirements. Step III, the definition of required performance results, will establish the output of the system. In Step IV, definition of the environmental specifications, the details of processing subsystems are developed. This is the major research step. Steps I through V utilize that research in the progressive construction and formulation of, first, the learning experience, and then the learning program within the environment. Once the preliminary design is in place, the entire package is validated in Step VI, and it is packaged, ready for consumption, in Step VII. A look at each step to see what is involved in its development will further clarify the process.

I. Define the Mission

The design process begins with a definition of the mission. The mission is a broad statement of what it is we hope to accomplish. The mission statement is broader in scope than an objective. It provides the framework within which specific objectives can be developed that will lead to the completion of the mission. For instance, the mission might be "win the war." The more specific objective of a field commander would be "take hill 73 by 0700 hours today." While the mission provides a framework, it also provides flexibility. The purpose of the mission statement is to provide a base, a reference point, for all future design decisions. To that end, the mission statement needs to specify what is to be done, with any imposed conditions, such as when, where, and at what cost. For example, our mission might be to: "Produce

Figure 10

Relationship of General Model to Design Process

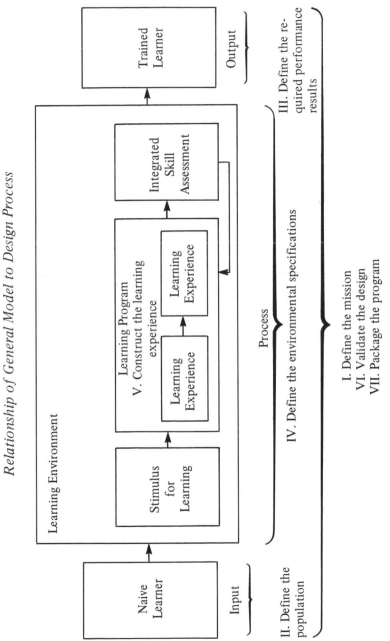

100 qualified store manager replacements." That is an acceptable statement. It tells us what must be done, and it imposes no conditions. Given that mission, we might elect to be creative by discarding our design role and by using a manager recruiter to satisfy the mission; and, as the mission is stated, this would be an acceptable method. Generally, as designers, we do not have the latitude to use *any* method to satisfy the mission. We have to operate under constraints. That being the case, the constraints need to be identified in the mission statement. Usually, these constraints fall into three categories: time, place, and cost. Developing our mission statement further to include these categories might produce the following statement: "Internally produce 100 qualified store manager replacements per year at a cost of no more than $5,000.00 each." In this mission statement, all of the categories that constrain our eventual design have been included.

- What is to be done?   Produce 100 qualified store
                          manager replacements
- Where (the place)?   Internally
- When (the time)?   Per year
- How much (the   No more than $5,000.00
  cost)?   per each

The general tendency of instructional designers is to attempt to confine and limit their flexibility at this point. This more than likely comes from the discipline we have forced upon ourselves in developing objectives. In writing a mission statement, however, this discipline works to our disadvantage. What we need here is a broad statement that, while identifying constraints, provides flexibility. For our purposes, at this stage the constraint of "internally" is far better than "put assistant managers in classroom training courses." The broad constraint of "per year" is more flexible than "26-week course." Therefore, while all restraints must be included, concerted efforts should be made to have them stated as broadly as possible. Otherwise, the design may be inadvertently dictated by the mission. Unless preconceived limitation is the intent, design flexibility should be retained until after the analysis has been completed.

II. Define the Population

More often than not, designers have little control over who is to be trained or educated. Typically, the learner is specified by some authority, such as the citizens of the community or the management in an enterprise. On a gross basis, certain prerequisites may be imposed upon learners entering the learning environment, but even then the designer will eventually need to design programs that will allow those who have been screened out to be screened in. Given that, the designer will have little control over designing the characteristics of the incoming naive learner. An alternative, then, is to understand and use the probable characteristics of those who will be placed in your program's charge.

The task in this second step is to analyze the probable population; to identify characteristics that will allow for the assumption of (1) the presence of skills or knowledge, and (2) the probable response of the learner. The assumed presence of a skill will have a major impact on the program design. An underlying assumption in LCI is that the learner will utilize past experience in reaching the learning objectives. Knowles (1970) draws a key distinction between pedology, the teaching of children, and andrology, the teaching of adults, by stating that "he (the adult) accumulates a growing reservoir of experience that becomes an increasing resource for learning." While Knowles makes a distinction between child learning and adult learning, it can be argued that it applies to all learning situations. As people, both young and old, enter a learning situation, they bring with them the effects of their prior behavioral conditioning. What is different is the amount of time they have been exposed to conditioning forces. The conditioning that takes place in the culture is not random. In *Beyond Freedom and Dignity,* Skinner (1971) says:

> In the scientific picture, a person is a member of a species shaped by evolutionary contingencies of survival, displaying behavior processes which bring him under the control of the environment which he and millions of others like him have constructed and maintained during the evolution of a culture.

We can, therefore, anticipate that individuals sharing a culture, individuals with like physical characteristics, and individuals who have shared the same experiences will generally have common responses to common stimuli. The predictability of acquired knowledge and probable response will be a valuable aid to the designer as he or she constructs the program.

The population analysis is geared to identifying similarities between individuals who are anticipated to enter the learning environment. Some of the similarities will be irrelevant. For example, a common language in a monolingual culture does not aid in categorizing the population. But, a common language in a bilingual culture would be a relevant character-istic. Characteristics are useful when they establish a subset within the population as a whole.

Three analytical frameworks are necessary in the develop-ment of the population analysis. They are:

   (a) demographic analysis;
   (b) subculture analysis; and
   (c) capability analysis.

Together these assist in categorizing the population for predictive purposes.

(a) Demographic Analysis
The demographic analysis is a review of vital statistics

relating to the population. These include, but are not limited to, data such as age, sex, educational attainment, marital status, income level, and military service. Knowing that a population is between 20 and 25 years of age provides vital information: they have had a lesser accumulation of experiences than a population of 45 to 50 years of age. For example, most learners between the ages of 20 to 25 are just starting work careers. They have different expectations about the future than do people in the age 45 to 50 bracket. The demographic analysis is easily displayed in a format similar to that shown in Figure 11.

The four columns in Figure 11 organize the essential elements of item, data, meaning, and use. For each item, there are one or more salient characteristics. Age, as shown in Figure 11, has only one salient characteristic, but age distribution could as easily be bi-modal with each mode generating its own set of major mission implications.

The mission implications are simply the designer's or analyst's interpretation of the meaning of the characteristic in relation to the mission. In this example, two such implications of the 20 to 25 year age characteristic are entry into a career and familiarity with youth values. Other implications could be generated by the analyst.

Lastly, the analyst looks at the implications to determine their use, i.e., their potential application in the program. At this stage in the analysis, it may be found that the implication is not useful. Usually, however, it will give direction to some aspect of program design. In the Figure 11 example, the educational attainment allows us to assume basic calculation skills that will be useful as we develop record keeping skills.

Data for the demographic analysis is generally the easiest to acquire. It is available from the basic personnel records that organizations maintain on students and employees.

Figure 11

Population Analysis Worksheet

POPULATION ANALYSIS WORKSHEET

MISSION: Internally produce 100 qualified store manager replacements at a cost of no more than $5,000.00 each.

---

1. Demographic Analysis

Item	Characteristic	Major Mission Implications	Potential Application in Program
Age	20-25	1. Entering career	1. Highly motivated. Will need minimum stimulus to enter program.
		2. Familiar with youth values	2. Use youth oriented learning resources and examples.

~~~

Educational attainment	1 yr. college	1. Rudimentary arithmetic skills	1. Can assume that no arithmetic training is needed for basic record keeping.

(b) Subculture Analysis

Subcultures are groups who exhibit characteristic patterns of behavior sufficient to distinguish them from others in the embracing culture or society. Subcultures include athletes, urbanites, Southerners, Northerners, soldiers, and so forth. By identifying the subcultures from which a population is drawn, it is once again possible to use the characteristics of those subcultures to assume experiences and predict responses.

Identification of subcultures is far more difficult than identification of demographic data. Usually, there are no files or records from which the data can be culled. This means the designer will need to identify items that may have some implications and utility, and then survey potential populations to determine if there are characteristics that lend themselves to use. For instance, if the mission involves producing marksmen, it is useful to know if the population is drawn from rural, urban, or combined subcultures. In this case, a population drawn from either subculture would allow assumptions about weapon familiarity that would be different from those that apply to the population in general. Once generated, the data can be displayed and developed on the population analysis worksheet in exactly the same manner as the demographic analysis.

(c) Capability Analysis

The last analysis in this set can be termed capability analysis. This analysis concerns itself with individual characteristics that may aid or impair learning. There are tools that can be used to aid in improving the learner's success in the program. Reading tests, dexterity tests, and physical and mental ability tests all measure the learner's capability to handle the program. If the mission involves heavy reading, the reading capabilities of the population are a useful bit of information. If physical stamina or problem-solving are keys to the accomplishment of the mission, then it is necessary to find out the extent to which these are characteristic of individuals in the entry population.

This phase of analysis is potentially the most difficult. It involves identifying characteristics that may have a bearing on both skill demonstration and learning, and then developing valid tests of learner capability. As with subculture analysis, random sampling is the most effective data collection technique. Once collected, the data can be displayed on the population analysis worksheet along with the other data. The same analysis of meaning and use can be applied to capability.

As population analysis is made, the framework of demographic, subculture, and capability will assist in data collection. The implications and potential applications of each characteristic can be displayed and organized on the population analysis worksheet. This definition of the population is a key step in building the LCI program. If the learner is to be in control, and if the designers are to be held responsible for designing an environment that will produce predictable learning results, the characteristics of the learner must be known. The designer must anticipate. The population must then be defined. The task is tedious but necessary. The rewards of the effort are visible only by their absence. Anticipated obstacles that fail to materialize are imaginary to most, but to the designer they are the awful reality that could have been.

III. Define the Required Performance Results

While the mission statement gives a broad description of direction, the required performance results more specifically define the outputs of the program. The mission statement does not assume "how" the mission is to be accomplished. Those responsible for the "how" accomplishments are free to choose any strategy within the specified conditions. The strategy might include a learning program. Then again, it might not. Required performance results focus on what a product of the environment must accomplish over time. These are the real-world performance measurements by which the program is measured. They are the criteria by which we determine, from a perspective of time, if the mechanisms we used to measure short-term learning accomplishments are effective. Further, they may tell us whether the measurements themselves are relevant. But they do not dictate a process by which the results are generated.

To state required performance results, we need to go to the next level of specificity from our mission statement. The statement must now take into account what is known about the population. The task in stating the required performance results, then, is identifying how the output or the product of the learning process will be different from the input.

The learning process is expected to change the behavior of those who enter it. That is the function of the process. If, as designers, we are to construct an efficient process, we begin by knowing what it will produce. Warren (1969), in speaking of training activities, has said:

> A real test of behavior change is how well the trainee performs in terms of task accomplishment. The only valid result of training or management development actions is a measurable increase or improvement in an individual's contribution to organizational goals.

Warren's position applies to both academic and industrial training. The organizational goals of industry and institutions of formal learning can be translated into the goals of society. In each case, the measure of learning program effectiveness is the change that is produced.

Depending on the scope and complexity of the mission, the required performance results may require one or a series of statements. Each statement should be self-contained. Each should describe: what the trained learner will be able to do, under what non-simulated conditions, and to what degree, *that the untrained learner could not do.* There are three key points in each statement:

(1) ability to do;
(2) under non-simulated conditions; and
(3) degree.

These points viewed from the perspective of the untrained learner will provide measuring points for evaluation of the instructional process and with guideposts for use in constructing that same process. Consider, for example, the mission of producing a number of master electricians from candidates who hold other full-time jobs. In this case, at least three statements of required performance results might be appropriate:

1. The learner will be able to pass the legislated master electrician examination on the initial try and gain certification.
2. The certified electrician will be able to secure employment as an electrician within three months after certification.
3. The employed, certified electrician will retain continuous employment for 12 months after initial hire.

These statements require performance in the real world. They require results. The learner must be able to "do," and that doing is in an environment no longer under the control of the designer. They are non-simulated. This example can be used to make an additional point. Training a learner in a skill involves more than learning that skill. It also involves training an individual in how to find application for the skill. If in a society or organization there is not opportunity for application of a skill or utilization of a knowledge, the design of a program that produces those skills or knowledges is a waste of resources.

Required performance results, therefore, focus on the output of the learning process. They identify those things the learner must accomplish after training. The statements contrast the input of the system against its output in terms that will allow evaluation of the design as well as direction for its construction.

IV. Define the Environmental Specifications

In LCI, the environment is a key resource. Assumptions made about the environment will greatly influence design decisions. If we define the environment as passive, i.e., not having an impact on the individual as learning occurs, then we will be required to build in events that consecrate our predictions of learning behavior. However, given recognition of an active environment, we can assume that the natural consequences will control behavior. Rousseau in *Emile* observed:

> Let (the student) believe that he is always in control, though it is always you (the teacher) who really controls. There is no subjugation so perfect as that which keeps the appearance of freedom, for in that way one captures volition itself. Can you not arrange everything in the world which surrounds him? Can you not influence him as you wish? His work, his play, his pleasures, his pains, are not all these in your hands and without his knowing it? Doubtless he ought to do only what he wants; but he ought to want to do only what you want him to do; he ought not to take a step which you have not predicted; he ought not open his mouth without your knowing what he will say.

Rousseau knew of the impact of the environment on the learner, but his ambition to predict may have outstripped his ability to control the environmental consequences. And few, if any, educators or trainers would want to exercise *that* degree of control over any human being. In contrast to Rousseau's declaration, the objectives in LCI are best served by trying to understand and use elements in the environment rather than to control them. As in any technology, use is a function of definition and understanding.

There are six steps involved in defining the environment. These steps make up the environmental analysis and provide the designer with a notion of how the environment will have an impact on learning. They are:

(a) specify major learning objectives;

(b) research potential learning experiences;

(c) specify entry criteria assumptions;

(d) specify framework of activities theory;

(e) specify consequence assumptions; and

(f) summarize the environmental assumptions.

At the point at which we begin definition of the environment, we have a fairly firm idea of the characteristics of the learner and the required results of the program. We know input and output requirements. Definition of the environment, therefore, will aid us in specifying the important characteristics that surround the processing or transformation of an incompetent to a competent performer.

(a) Specify Major Learning Objectives

The first step in the process of defining the environment is, of course, a detailed specification of all major learning objectives. Mager (1962), in *Preparing Instructional Objectives,* establishes the framework for specification:

> An objective is an intent communicated by a statement describing a proposed change in the learner—a statement of what the learner is to be like when he has successfully completed a learning experience. It is a description of a pattern of behavior we want the learner to be able to demonstrate.
>
> ... the best statement is the one that excludes the greatest number of possible alternatives to your goal.

Specification of objectives in LCI is no less important than the same specification in any other instructional mode. It may be that because of the flexibility of action in LCI, the objectives are even more important.

The objectives developed at this stage should clearly communicate the intended learning outcome. They will form the framework around which the rest of your environmental definition will be displayed. They provide the starting points for analysis.

More likely than not, there will be several objectives. Each will focus on a major element of the program. In the Allied Store Management LCI Program (Wydra, 1968), for example, 23 major objectives were specified. The Sherwin Williams Program (Creative Universal, 1975) specified 49 objectives. While the subject of each objective in each program differed, they were all designed to accomplish the mission by producing the required outcomes. To illustrate, one major objective in the Allied program was that learners would "recognize, on sight, all standard retail cuts of meat and identify the primal cut from which they were produced." Another was, "prepare a work schedule to accomplish the store work load within the dollar, percentage, and productivity limits set by the division." Product recognition and labor scheduling are two dissimilar skills. Their common characteristics, however, are that they are both necessary for accomplishment of the mission and, of course, the production of the required performance results. Another characteristic which they share is that they could each represent the terminal objective of a discrete learning program.

In Learner Controlled Instruction, the learner will frequently be working toward the accomplishment of several objectives concurrently. When progress or interest in one objective wanes, the learner will decide to switch to an alternate objective. The variety that allows choice is a hallmark of LCI. The flexibility to allow this choice must be built in at the environmental level. It is here that the interrelationship of objectives required to achieve a common mission is identified. For example, having specified the major objectives of perishable product recognition and labor scheduling in the Allied program, the constraints on the learning environment began to take shape. Product recognition and labor scheduling both suggest a dynamic environment, one that changes continuously to allow the formation of generalizations and discriminations. In this situation, three alternatives for selection of a physical learning environment present themselves: a classroom, a simulated environment, or a real-world environment. While the objectives could be taught in a classroom, they need to be demonstrated in a dynamic environment. Therefore, either of the two latter alternatives would be a better choice for the locale of learning in a LCI program. In the case of the store manager program, it was eventually decided that a retail store was the best physical environment for learning. It is important to note, though, that the physical environment was chosen after the major objectives were specified—and not before. It is better to identify the objectives and then look for environments that provide minimum inhibition and maximum support to the learning process.

Thus, specification of learning objectives must be the first step in the process of defining the environment. The objectives that are specified provide the framework for the remainder of the definition.

(b) Research Potential Learning Experiences

The second step of environmental definition is to research the potential learning experiences. For every skill, there is a variety of ways in which it can be acquired. On the most basic level, each skill can be acquired randomly from the environment. On the other hand, a learning program can be constructed to direct and speed that acquisition. Learning programs are, after all, nothing more than mechanisms that substitute structured experience for random experience. The objective of the structure is to reduce acquisition time. Nonetheless, even at the basic level, learning can take place under either of two conditions: random or structured experience. An English-speaking person can learn to speak French by being placed in a French-speaking environment or by taking structured French lessons. Eventually, both will learn to use some French words. The important point is to recognize that there is a variety of ways to learn things.

For each major objective, the designer must identify the potential learning experiences. Sometimes, the skills will be rudimentary enough so that an option will be to learn directly from the environment. Other skills, such as distinguishing between various forms of bacteria or flying a jet aircraft, will rarely be learned solely as a result of interacting with the environment. Regardless of the level of the skill or knowledge, a designer's task at this stage is to identify potential sources to be used later in transferring knowledge. Since we are dealing with "potential" sources, we want to include, rather than exclude, experience. The base question to ask is, how and where could this knowledge be acquired?

Taking our French language example a bit further, we might uncover a variety of potential learning experiences:

Objective	*Potential Learning Experiences*
To carry on a 15-minute conversation with a French-speaking person	1. Live in a French-speaking community.
	2. Attend French speech classroom instruction.
	3. Use French speech audio training program.
	4. Tune in to TV morning French lessons.
	5. Use French speech tutor.
	6. Read an instructional manual on French speech.
	7. Study bilingual dictionary.

Some of these potential learning experiences will be practical, others impractical, but all will have the capability of allowing the transfer of knowledge.

The specification of potential learning experiences also helps us further define the environment. Foreign language communities are, normally, associated with distant places. Given financial resources, we could transport our learner to such a place, but given a broad definition of community, we might find individual businesses or families that use the foreign language as their primary communication mode. To stretch the point—but also to make it—if speaking French were a requirement of the store manager training program mentioned earlier, then the environment of training could be a retail food store in Montreal, Canada.

More likely, an objective to speak French will be an academic requirement. One of the teaching tactics often used is to create a simulated French-speaking community through the establishment of inhibitions on non-French language used during certain times of the day. The eventual environment will be defined by the creativity the designer displays in defining the potential learning experience. Had we excluded the potential experience of living in a foreign language community, we would not have developed the environmental assumptions to allow consideration of using a real or simulated transfer mechanism.

As a list of potential learning experiences is developed, focus is on the previously defined major objectives, and the task is inclusion rather than exclusion of experiences. It is useful to list each objective on a separate 5 x 7 card and to list the potential learning experiences that apply on the same card. In this way, the experiences can be added to without major revision of a format. Further, such display will allow cross comparison of potential experiences. The comparison will make identification of the most efficient physical environments an easier task.

(c) Specify Entry Criteria Assumptions

The third step in the process of defining the environment is to specify the entry criteria assumptions. The population has previously been defined. Now, that definition needs to be synthesized into a set of assumptions to guide specification of criteria for entry into the program. Note that at this step we are focusing on entry into the program, while in a later step we will look at criteria for entry into specific learning paths. For now, though, we will take a microscopic view of entry requirements.

Because of the flexibility of the LCI design, the entry requirements are generally less rigorous than those used in other models. Learners will have a variety of options throughout the program. Consequently, the learner is often able to overcome shortcomings by taking alternate learning paths or by simply spending more time at points of difficulty.

There are two major concerns that a designer must be aware of as entry criteria are established:

1. Are there any identifiable characteristics of the learner that would prevent the learner from utilizing the learned skills *after* completion of the program?

2. Are there any identifiable characteristics of the learner that make failure to complete the program highly probable?

If either of these conditions exists, the design specifications should prohibit entry for individuals having these specified characteristics. If, for example, legislation has established age, height, or physical requirements for people who can practice a skill, then such requirements must be included as entry criteria. Sixteen-year-olds might be able to learn the art of bartending, but if legislation establishes a minimum age requirement for bartending that is greater than 16 years old, this should be clearly established as an entry criterion.

Learner characteristics that would almost insure failure

must also be specified. If, in the identification of the potential learning experience, it appears that heavy reliance will be placed on reading skills, then an entry criterion should be established that assesses the learner's reading capability. If a major objective requires color discrimination, then color acuity must be established as an entry criterion. If the criterion is not established, the learner will fail, and the failure will have been caused by poor design.

A well-designed LCI program will allow success for most learners. Those learners, however, whose failure, either during or after the program, is predictable should be screened out. The specification of the mechanism for such screening is the responsibility of the designer.

(d) Specify Framework of Activities Theory

The fourth specification needed for definition of the environment is the theory to be used in establishing the framework of learner activities. This is one of the most critical of the design steps. It is here that the designer will outline the decisions he or she intends to delegate to the learner and the constraints he or she will impose upon the learner.

There are any number of decisions that can be delegated to the learner, but five seem to demand special attention. These are the decisions concerning objectives, sequence, pace, presentation mode, and evaluation. The designers will need to determine the extent to which each of these is delegated. Together, these decisions will establish the theory of a viable program.

1. *Who decides objectives?* The first decision that can be considered for delegation is the determination of the objective. In essence, this decision concerns deciding what the goal of the learning experience should be. In discussions of LCI, it often comes up that this is thought to be the primary decision controlled by the learner. Reference is often made

to the Sumnerhill experiment in Britain and the British Open Schools to show that the learner should decide the objective of learning. It is held that the motivation to learn is a function of the freedom one is given in choosing subjects of learning. There may be some validity to this position in cases of a well-informed learner operating in a traditional learning environment. In this case, the learning programs are linear, and the learner, if he or she is knowledgeable enough to make the choice, has already learned something about the goals.

In more complex learning strategies, such as LCI, however, there are several valid reasons not to delegate the decision of the objective to the learner. The first and most important reason is that the designer assumes and states objectives as part of the design process. The structure of the program is then shaped to produce responses on the part of the learner to meet the objectives. The learner's decision, then, knowing the objective, is to enter the program or not. Since the structure of the program has been designed to produce the prespecified objectives, change of the objectives within the program would make the program a non-program. Instead, the learner would be using the resources at random with little or no predictability of outcomes.

A second argument against delegation of objectives is that the learner does not have the perspective to distinguish between short-term and long-term consequences of learning. With limited knowledge of long-term use or importance, the learner may neglect important learning objectives that have long-term but not short-term consequences. Often, in complex learning situations, it is the interrelationship of several disciplines that produces the final objective. Without the recognition to gauge this impact, the learner may reach the apparent final stages of a program only to be frustrated by a poor objective selection early in the program. For these reasons, although it is possible to delegate decisions concerning objectives, I would counsel against it in LCI designs.

2. *Who decides the sequence?* Sequencing offers a count-er-balance to objectives. The decision of objectives addresses the question of "Where am I going?" Sequencing a decision assumes an answer and then addresses the question of "Which path will I follow?"

In linear programs, the determination of path is always decided by the designer. One piece of information is consistently presented after another. This sequence is fol-lowed in individualized linear programs, such as programmed self-instruction, as well as group linear programs, such as a lecture series. In either case, the learner does not and can not make decisions about sequence.

Learner Controlled Instruction, by its very nature, is a non-linear concept. It assumes that there will be decision points and that there will be multiple objectives and multiple learning paths for each objective. The decision the designer needs to make, then, is not whether to delegate sequencing but, instead, to what degree. In forming the theory of the program, the designer needs to decide the degree to which the paths are made visible to the learner. The more visible the paths, the more documentation needed for learning progress.

On one hand, the designer may elect to define only the objectives, resources, and measurements and let the learner find his or her way through the program. In this theory of sequencing, the learner has an opportunity to randomly use the resources to reach the objective. The designer in this case would not offer any visible structure to the course. The other extreme (Horn *et al.,* 1971) is a fully documented program with learning and information maps on every objective and resource. As learning maps are provided, the visible structure of the program is increased.

Some environments, nonetheless, lend themselves admira-bly to structure in sequencing. A LCI course in which all resources are contained in a reference library is easily mapped. The same course becomes more difficult to map or definitively structure as dynamic resources, such as real-life events or people, are added.

The order of events within a path needs to be considered, too. For a learning objective that involves basic arithmetic skills, the decision needs to be made as to whether division or multiplication is to be learned first. If these decisions are made by the designer, the structure will be increased.

It should be noted, though, that structure is not an evil. Structure directs the learning and is assumed to produce the most efficient use of a resource. But, that very structure limits options. As a general rule, the designer should increase the structure surrounding sequencing as the program becomes more complex. However, the minimum structure of sequencing needed to insure achievement of the objectives is the most desirable.

The resources identified in the research of potential learning experiences and the limitations of the entry criteria will serve as a guide to the amount of sequencing delegation to be built into the program. As a guide to sequencing decisions, these factors, already discussed, should be considered:

Factors that Decrease Delegation of Sequencing Decision Potential	*Factors that Increase Delegation of Sequencing Decision Potential*
* Linear Construction	* Non-Linear Construction
* Complexity of Program Content Design	* Simplicity of Program Content Design
* Abundance of Documentation	* Sparseness of Documentation
* Static Resources	* Dynamic Resources
* Scarcity of Events in a Path	* Variety of Events in a Path
* Assumption about Learner	* Assumption about Learner

3. *Who will set the pace?* The question of pacing is also a key in establishing the theory of the framework. Pacing is the speed at which the learner moves toward the objective. A mile runner will pace himself or herself differently from the speed merchant who runs the 100-yard dash. Learners, too, may travel at different rates in their movement to the finish line. Some may proceed at a steady, consistent pace. Others may travel in bursts alternated with pauses. Still others may delay starting but then put forth prodigious effort near the end of the course. In these examples, there is a differing pace within the course, but all learners are expected to complete the total course in a prescribed time. All learners are expected to "peak" at the point in time when the instructor makes the final evaluation, usually through examination.

What is not easily accommodated are learners whose pace is so slow that they do not complete the course objectives by evaluation time. The assumption is, therefore, that they have not learned. The assumption is not valid. Slow pace is not equivalent to lack of learning. The situation where individuals learn quickly is another one that is handled poorly. Those who "peak" early are left to their own devices, including boredom and mischief, to fill the gap. In either case, the problem is a function of the pacing decision being made by the wrong person, the instructor.

In an instructor controlled program, theoretically, two activities take place simultaneously. The instructor makes information available; the learner gains mastery over the information. In reality, each of these activities may proceed on independent schedules. The instructor presents information on the schedule dictated by the lesson plan. The learner gains mastery through drill and practice. Given all of the information, the learner may be a pacer or a sprinter, but the "catch" is that learners are not usually given all of the information. It is released on the schedule established by the instructor. This usually prevents learners from getting "too far ahead."

The degree to which self-pacing can be delegated, there-fore, is the function of the availability of information, and in some cases, experience. The learner cannot move at a pace faster than that which information becomes available. If the information is instructor bound, i.e., if it can only be released by an instructor, then the instructor has control over the pace. In addition to being instructor bound, information access may be restricted by other factors. For instance, events that are critical to the learning process may only become available sequentially or periodically. Learning how to ski requires snow. The learners who cannot travel to the snow must wait for the snow to come to them. This is a periodic event and the time length between periods is a function of geography.

The potential learning experiences researched in the second step of the environmental definition are the best guides to the availability of information. If the experiences are contingent upon the presence of a person or event, the availability is restricted. In the example used earlier, concern-ing learning to speak French, some of the experiences were quite restricted. Using a French tutor, attending a French speech class, and tuning to televised French lessons are all limited to availability of information. If these were the only experiences available, the decision to delegate pacing would be severely affected. The identification of other experiences, such as use of a French-speaking audio training program, expands the availability of information. As a result, delega-tion of the pacing decision becomes possible.

Availability of information establishes the fastest potential track through the program. The slowest track is a function of the evaluation mechanism and administrative tolerance. Evaluation mechanisms that work against self-pacing are, like information sources, those that are controlled by an event or person other than the learner. Typically, these mechanisms are tests that only partially measure achievement or those that require interpretive "judgment" on the part of the appraiser. The partial measurement implies a random sampling of achievement. If the sample items become known through premature exposure, it damages their reliability as measurement tools. Access to the evaluation mechanism is, therefore, restricted to learners, except at fixed points in time. Interpretive judgment by definition assumes flexible measurement criteria. Consequently, the timing of such judgment is controlled by the interpreting expert. Mechanisms that allow full measurement of skill and knowledge required, with little or no interpretation, free themselves from time constraints.

A more serious restraint on pacing is administrative tolerance. In industrial as well as in academic learning programs, individuals are assessed not only on what they have learned but also on the speed or quickness of learning. The reasons for this are easy to see. Academic programs are geared to processing large numbers of people. Allowing slow learners to disrupt schedules has an impact on the entire system and makes it less efficient. In industrial programs, the problem is compounded because not only would there be a disruption of schedules, but also the cost is increased. Learners in industrial programs are generally paid while in training. The longer the learning program, the greater the cost. As schedules are disrupted and costs are increased, administrative tolerance for slow learners is diminished.

The decision to delegate pacing decisions to the learner must include an explanation of the limit of administrative tolerance. Since we can expect individual learners to move through different paths and sequences at different rates, we can also expect that there will be give-and-take within the course. However, completion of the total program often hinges on the timely completion of key tasks. Two situations can occur. One is that the learner may have completed all the objectives but one; work on the remaining objective continues, but the learner is underutilized in total. The other situation is that learning progresses steadily but at a rate slower than that of other learners. The quality is there but not the speed. In these situations, the learner must know the limit of administrative tolerance. Otherwise, the organization may eliminate the learner from the learning environment before the learner has eliminated the learning deficiencies.

All in all, delegation of pacing decisions establishes constraints on the type of learning resources used, the nature of the evaluation mechanisms, and the limit of administrative tolerance. As pacing is delegated, information access must be increased and evaluation mechanisms must be refined. Otherwise, the pacing decision remains in the power of those who control information dissemination, evaluation, and administrative time limits.

4. *Who decides how the information will be presented?* If the objective is where we are going, and sequencing is the path to be followed, and pacing is the speed along the path, then presentation mode is the vehicle that takes us from point to point.

In establishing the theory of the program, presentation mode will restrict or expand program flexibility concerning physical location. In addition, the array of presentation options made available to the learner will determine the degree of choice he or she exercises. Consequently, it is useful to determine the alternatives that will be employed before constructing exercises.

Presentation mode is being used here to mean the mechanism that transfers information from the source to the learner. Lectures, written materials, videotapes, and filmstrips are different modes of presentation. Certain presentation modes lend themselves to LCI programs; others do not. Therefore, parameters need to be established at the planning stage to insure that idealism does not overwhelm practicality.

probable that a variety of presentation modes is in evidence. Their application to LCI, however, can be evaluated using three criteria:

(a) the degree to which the mode is learner operated;

(b) the sophistication or complexity of operation; and

(c) the portability of presentation modes.

Presentations that require operation by a person other than the learner place a dependency upon the operator by the learner. To the extent that the learner cannot selectively turn the presentation of information on or off, his or her control is lost. A lecturer controls his or her own presentation. He or she is not learner operated. However, videotape the lecturer, turn the apparatus over to the learner, and the learner can control the presentation.

Sophisticated or complex presentation equipment that requires either an operator other than the learner or extended time periods for training in operation reduces its utility for LCI. If, for example, the videotape machine is so complex or sophisticated that it requires a trained technician to operate, then nothing is gained by videotaping the lecture. We are still limited by the operator. Another example would be a computerized instructional lesson that would require extensive learner orientation before it could be utilized. The orientation might be worthwhile if there were many potential applications within the course, but if its use is limited, then the effort required is greater than the reward. Consider, for instance, the learner who spends eight hours learning to manipulate a presentation mode to gain access to a lesson that takes eight hours. If this same information would take 17 or more hours to present by other mechanisms, then there is a net gain for the learner. However, if the same data could effectively be presented in fewer than 16 hours, it would establish an argument against the use of the computer. Therefore, the characteristics of the equipment have an effect on the presentation mode. More importantly, these characteristics have the potential of frustrating the intent of the designer, unless they are considered as part of the theory of the program.

Finally, the portability of learning resources must be considered. Portability refers to the learner's ability to move the presentation device from place to place. A book is portable, a lectern less so. Some presentation devices are large, or bulky, or connected and, therefore, difficult to move. If many of the available presentation devices are fixed in one location, the theory of design will need to accommodate placement of the learner. The degree of portability inherent in the presentation vehicle will control both location and time of presentation. Consequently, sequence and pace as well as the physical locus of learning become a function of presentation mode portability.

Non-portable presentation devices are usually placed in locations where there are large concentrations of learners. This makes sense because these devices are usually expensive. Their placement near learners increases utilization and, therefore, decreases per unit cost. In a LCI program, the design strategy is usually to place the learner in an experiential environment. The learner is to be placed in the real world where the non-contrived consequences can have an impact on the learning behaviors. This, in turn, means that most, or all, of the presentation devices must be portable enough to accompany the learner to the learning environment. As a general rule, the more portable the presentation device, the more it will lend itself to the LCI design. If, in review of potential learning experiences, it is discovered that most presentation devices are non-portable, the theory of the program will be directly affected.

In summary, operation, complexity, and portability are the characteristics of presentation mode that will most influence the theory of the program. The modes that lend themselves to LCI application are those that can be operated by a learner at his or her own discretion, those that are simple rather than complex, and those that are mobile. The degree to which these characteristics are present in the potential learning experiences will determine the applicability of the program to the LCI design strategy.

5. *Who will evaluate results?* The final issue in establishing the theoretical framework of the program is evaluation. Following the analogy we have used thus far, evaluation is the measurement used to tell us when we have arrived. The decision of the designer to delegate or retain the evaluation decision is potentially the most controversial. Evaluation has long been the province of the instructor. The teacher's power to assess performance and award grades has been an effective control mechanism. This power has been used to selectively reinforce learning behaviors and accomplishments. Evaluators have built a science out of the assessment of achievement and the awarding of marks. Grades have been awarded against a standard, on a curve, and even on a non-graded basis. The issue has always been the appropriate labeling of an achievement so that others can correctly interpret the degree of skill of a learner. Along the way, evaluators found that grades were sometimes effective reinforcers of study behavior. Generally, those individuals who studied diligently performed well on final achievement tests and, therefore, received high marks. The more perceptive instructors learned that under such a scheme only the terminal behavior was reinforced. The many learners who had not built a chain of study behavior leading to adequate terminal behavior were not reinforced. The reinforcement chain was too long and evaluations lost their effect as reinforcers. To shorten the chain, periodic evaluations, such as those based on performance at fixed and random points, were introduced. Mid-term examinations, spot quizzes, and the like provided the instructor with the ability to aid in both the assessment and reinforcement of learner activity. Activity, though, is not accomplishment.

By and large, the periodic evaluation was a useful improvement. It gave learners feedback on the standards of the instructor; this then could be used to alter behavior. For the instructor or trainer, though, this scheme created problems of resource allocation. The resource is time. An evaluation of the learner's comprehension of all material presented would require examination time equal to learning time. Further, the results of examinations needed to be evaluated and fed back to the learner. In instructional settings where one teacher handles multiple learners, time runs out too soon.

To optimize the situation, instructors have tried to balance instructional versus evaluation time. The main tool in their effort has been the concept of basing evaluations on only a sample of performance. The theory here is that if the sample of a learner's behavior is valid, it will be representative of total behavior. Consequently, the evaluation mode on the sample will validly apply to the whole.

As we follow this line of reasoning, it becomes evident that if the sample is to be valid, it needs to be independent of learner control. Samples that can be manipulated by the learner become invalid and do not, therefore, represent total behavior. For example, learners who are aware of the items from the set that will constitute the sample may concentrate on learning only those items from which the sample of knowledge is drawn. It will appear that the learners have mastered all items in the set when, in fact, the only mastery is of the sample subset items. To prevent learners from manipulating the sample, instructors have gone to great lengths to keep the sample items, or examination points, secret.

To trace this all back and put it in perspective, teachers have found that grades are conditioned reinforcers that increase accomplishment. They have also found that accomplishment is a function of diligent study habits. Therefore, they have concluded that interim reinforcing evaluations will help build lasting study habits. A dilemma arises in balancing time available for instruction with time available for evaluation. Consequently, samples of behavior are used to assess total behavior. To maintain the integrity of the sample and prevent its manipulation by the learner, it is kept secret. Now, reversing the path, we only need secrecy when we use a sample. We only need a sample when evaluation competes in time with instruction. Competition for time occurs only when the instructor both instructs and evaluates. Instructors need to evaluate only when they are the only subject matter experts who can evaluate accomplishment. Finally, evaluations only need to be made if they are reinforcing and allow feedback to the learner and unambiguous accomplishment data to other interested parties.

These points become important as the framework of the program is developed.

The designer will need to decide whether and to what extent the evaluation decision should be delegated to the learner. This decision hinges on two factors:

(1) where the subject matter expertise resides; and

(2) the extent to which the universe of expected accomplishment will be tested.

When the subject matter expertise resides only in the minds of people, then only they can make evaluations of performance. The evaluation by a gymnastic judge is subjective. It deals with form as much as substance. The expertise needed to make discriminations resides within a person, the judge. Fortunately for us, most evaluations are a matter of substance and procedure rather than form. The points of discrimination between acceptable and unacceptable performance have been categorized. They can be recognized as present or absent by comparison to a standard. If the skills and knowledges to be learned can be measured against a standard that can be interpreted by the learner, then it is possible to delegate the evaluation decision. Evaluation of procedure and result in math training can be delegated because of the predictability of results when a set procedure is followed. In other words, the standard is fixed; right versus wrong can be evaluated by comparison against a set standard.

The second factor that goes into the evaluation delegation decision is the comprehensiveness of the test. Tests of accomplishment that retain their validity with full learner knowledge of measurements and standards lend themselves to delegation. The test of jumping skills is the height or length of the jump under certain conditions. In a broad or long jump, marks in the sand bed measure the start and finish of the jump. A ruler fixes the distance. Even though the measuring devices and standards are known, they cannot be manipulated by the performer. A spelling examination in which words are presented over a tape recorder and checked against a written display allows total rather than random testing. The testing can be evaluated by the learner. However, when we begin to selectively test, when the test represents a sample, when that sample requires secrecy, then the delegation decision is inhibited.

Whenever possible, evaluation should be delegated in a LCI program. Self-evaluation allows the learner pertinent, timely feedback on performance that can be used to alter sequence, pace, path, and content. The decision to delegate or retain power to evaluate performance must be built into the basic framework of the program. The problems of evaluation delegation need to be thought through in the conceptual stage of design. Should the overall decision be to delegate this authority, then the designer must insure that the subject matter expertise is proceduralized and that the testing of accomplishment is adequate.

The evaluation decision is the last delegation to be discussed in the specification of the framework of learner activities theory. Specification of the theory is a key step in the definition of the learning environment. It follows and complements the steps of specification of major learning objectives, researching potential learning experiences, and specification of the entry criteria assumptions.

The purpose for the development of the framework of learner activities theory is to establish the conceptual base for delegation of key learning decisions. Within the theory, five major delegations of authority decisions have been addressed. They are decisions concerning control of:

(a) establishing objectives;

(b) sequence;

(c) pace;

(d) presentation mode; and

(e) evaluation of learning.

Once the theory of learner activities is set, it should be verbalized. Each decision should be made visible and specified on a worksheet. The designer must identify each decision he or she expects the learner to make and those that will be made by the designer or someone else. The process of thinking through and committing to each of these decisions will aid the designer in handling each design element. In addition, the decision guide will serve as a useful reference tool for review of the design prior to and during the validation procedure. The theory sets the framework for learner activities. It establishes the overall concept that will guide the design plan. It also sets the stage for the specification of the assumptions about the consequences that exist in the learning environment.

(e) Specify Consequence Assumptions

We now know quite a bit about the eventual program that will emerge. By this point, our concept of the eventual physical environment of learning should be taking shape. The definition of major learning objectives, the potential learning experiences, entry criteria assumptions, and the theory of learner activities have all served to restrict the environment in which learning is possible. Only one, two, or perhaps several types of environments will still accommodate learning. However, before the final decision as to environment is made, any assumptions concerning consequences that will control and direct learning need to be identified.

Behavior is controlled by its consequences. Learning is but one of a number of processes that involve changing behaviors. As learning occurs, behavior is emitted and altered by consequences. Predictability of consequences, therefore, is central to predictability of learning behavior.

In a traditional learning environment, we rely on the teacher or coach to provide the learner with feedback or cues to the eventual effects of emitted behavior when the message is not directly obvious from immediate consequences in the environment. In a learner controlled environment, on the other hand, the teacher or coach is absent. The feedback, therefore, needs to be built into the environment.

The science of behavior, as it exists today, has not developed to the point where all behaviors are predictable, nor is the effect of all consequences known. It is not likely that they ever will be, but even with the state of the art as it is, it is possible to make educated guesses about both behavior and the probable effect of consequences, if we have some knowledge about previous behavior patterns.

People who live in environments for extended time periods learn the long-term consequences of an action. A suburban gardener watering his or her lawn each day will not see the effects of the watering immediately. Over time, though, he or she will find that the water either encourages growth or builds a weak root system which makes the grass susceptible to damage. A possible positive or negative consequence is present. Only time will teach him or her. To the gardener, the grass looks fresher after a watering. That is usually viewed as a positive change. To the gardener, the grass seems to have grown more vigorously after watering, another positive change. However, the immediate and intermediate effect of daily, *shallow* watering may mask a negative, long-term consequence, shallow root production. Unless an individual has lived in the environment for a prolonged period, he or she may be deceived by the short-term effects of his or her actions.

In a LCI environment, a learner working without guidance from a coach may allow short-time effects to mask long-term consequences. To avoid this, it is imperative that the designer be thoroughly familiar with the environment in which learning will occur. It is also important for the designer to have the power to alter consequences within the environment that could distort learning. Lacking that, the designer must at least be aware of those situations and build in counter-feedback mechanisms that will allow learners to adjust their behavior.

To aid in the analysis of consequences in the environment and to their specification, the Learning Environment Selection Worksheet is a useful tool. The worksheet, shown in Figure 12, provides a format that organizes key data needed to specify consequences and to assist in the selection of learning environments.

Using this format, the major objectives which the designer has already developed are simply noted in the first column. For each major objective, one or more separate skills may be involved. Each separate skill which is considered significant is then listed in the second column. For example, the major objective of learning to operate a forklift truck will involve the skills shown in Figure 13.

Normal demonstrations (the third and fourth columns of Figure 12) can now be explored and introduced to the chart. Each skill can be learned and demonstrated in isolation from the others. Each may even have a separate physical location or environment of performance. To continue the forklift example, the skills of driving and fork manipulation may be

Figure 12

Learning Environment Selection Worksheet Sample

Major Objective	Skills to Be Demonstrated	Normal Demonstration		Unique Consequences of Demonstration				Potential Learning Experiences	Learning Environment	
		Environment	Frequency	Correctly Performed		Incorrectly Performed			Primary	Secondary
				Short-term	Long-term	Short-term	Long-term			

LEARNING ENVIRONMENT SELECTION WORKSHEET

Figure 13

Segment of Learning Environment Selection Worksheet

		Learning	
		Normal Demonstrat	
Major Objective	Skills to Be Demonstrated	Environment	Fre
Operate a forklift truck	1. Starting, driving, stopping 2. Manipulating fork 3. Servicing 4. Preventive maintenance		

normally demonstrated in the stock room of a warehouse. Preventive maintenance skills, however, are usually demonstrated in the maintenance areas. This means that this particular objective could be completely demonstrated in a warehouse environment even though two areas are involved. This is usually the case in skill demonstrations that focus on a particular job. Academic subjects, however, may require greater diversity of environment. Regardless, the identification of normal performance location will aid in the identification of important consequences that are linked to the environment.

The frequency of normal demonstration for each skill is also a useful bit of information in assessing consequences. An event that occurs every seven minutes is more likely to take place during the learning period than is one that occurs every seven hours. Here the old rule of behaviorists applies: behaviors must be emitted to be consequenced. The more frequently a behavior occurs, the more available it is for shaping. Less frequent displays may require special attention to create situations that will elicit opportunities for skill demonstrations. Demonstration frequency is, therefore, directly linked to consequence frequency and needs identification. In the example we have been using, driving a forklift truck and the manipulation of the forks may be demonstrated on a more or less continuous basis in the normal environment. Servicing by recharging batteries and adding water is done on a daily basis, while preventive maintenance tasks are normally done on a weekly basis. With these bits of information displayed, we can now fill in the key data about consequences as illustrated in Figure 14.

Unique Consequences of Demonstration (the fifth through eighth columns) really mean unique, visible consequences of demonstration in a normal environment. There may be many consequences resulting from demonstration of the skill, but not all need to be recorded. For our purposes, only those

Figure 14

Segment of Learning Environment Selection Worksheet

LEARNING ENVIRONMENT SELECTION WORKSHEET

Major Objective	Skills to Be Demonstrated	Normal Demonstration		Unique Consequences of Demonstration			
		Environment	Frequency	Correctly Performed		Incorrectly Performed	
				Short-term	Long-term	Short-term	Long-term
Operate a forklift truck	1. Starting, driving, stopping	Warehouse stock room	Continuous	None	None	No or erratic movement	None
	2. Manipulating fork	Warehouse stock room	Continuous	None	None	Stock damaged, topping	None
	3. Servicing	Maintenance room	Daily	Vehicle operator	None	Vehicle does not operate	None
	4. Preventive Maintenance	Maintenance room	Weekly	None	Vehicle operator	None	Vehicle does not operate

that can be interpreted by the learner and those that can be directly related to performance are important, i.e., those consequences that are visible and unique. A further categorization of demonstration is whether or not it was correctly executed. Sometimes there are visible, direct consequences regardless of the correctness of the demonstration. However, most of the time there will only be a visible consequence in one but not both of the situations. For instance, in this example, there is no notable direct, unique consequence to correctly starting, driving, and stopping a forklift truck. The effect of such action on the stock room floor would go unnoticed. However, incorrect skill demonstration on the part of the learner will cause a visible, direct, short-term change in the environment; the forklift truck will be immobile, erratic, or unstable. In most warehouses, such demonstration will bring high visibility to the performance of the learner.

In addition, the effect of performance can have both a short-term and a long-term consequence. When the consequence becomes visible, it is extremely important to use it as a control mechanism in the environment. The servicing of a vehicle will have an immediate short-term consequence. It will or will not operate, depending on whether or not the battery is recharged. This can be used as an internal program consequence. The consequence of performing preventive maintenance, on the other hand, is long-term. It will be less visible; therefore, it needs to be noted. In these cases, the designer will need to build in controls other than those that exist in the normal environment to guide and direct learner performance.

By displaying the consequences that exist in the natural environment, the designer is in a better position to judge which consequences will guide the learner performance. Using the identified consequences that have been specified in the environment or environments in which learning will occur, the designer now needs to determine if effective alternatives and additional consequences can be built in. For each skill to be demonstrated, there must be a short-term consequence that is interpretable by the learner. The short-term consequence may either be a reinforcing stimulus for correct performance or an aversive stimulus for incorrect performance. However, one or the other must be present and they must be short-term. The learner has no other feedback that will allow correct interpretation of conflicting short-term and long-term effects. Therefore, the short-term consequence must be present, and it must be accurate. If a void exists, the designer must decide if a simulated consequence or feedback mechanism can be contrived. If none can be contrived, then the designer must turn to an alternative environment.

This is a crucial decision. The natural environment of performance is the most desirable, but without short-term consequences that accurately cue long-term consequences, the natural environment should be avoided. The next most desirable environment is one that simulates the natural. Once more, the analysis of consequences should be made. If again the simulated consequences cannot be constructed, then the only alternative is use of instructor controlled consequences. The designer's specifications in this step will guide the decision in construction and will eventually help in insuring that the learner is successful.

(f) Summarize the Environmental Assumptions

The last step in the process of defining the environmental specifications is to summarize them and select primary and secondary environments. By this time, the task should be fairly easy. Objectives, potential learning experiences, entry criteria assumptions, framework of activities theory, and consequence assumptions have all been made visible. The job now is to put it together piece by piece.

The primary environment is home base for the learner. It is the place where, or set of controlled conditions under which, the designer would like learning to take place. This environment needs to be identified for each major objective. There will be a primary environment for each learning activity and for the program as a whole. These may be different. Generally, though, they will be the same. In the LCI training program that covered Retail Management Skills, the primary environment was a retail store. Most learning activities took place in that environment because it was the eventual environment of performance. Some learning and real-life activities, however, were best performed out of the store. Competitive price checking is one example. For this activity, a competitor's store became the primary learning environment. That is where the real-life performance occurs.

Typically, the primary learning environment will be the place where the skill will normally be performed. This, though, is not always possible or practical. The normal performance area for public speakers is a public assembly, but people do not predictably assemble without a purpose. When they do, they usually have an agenda that would act to discourage use of the assembly as a learning environment for fledgling orators. Therefore, as a practical matter, we replace the public assembly with a simulated assembly. There may be other learners who trade off time for reciprocal use of the assembly as a learning resource, or the simulation may be a videotape of listeners. In either case, it is a simulation. The simulation will occur at some physical location. That location becomes the primary environment for learning.

The secondary environment is an alternate place where learning can occur if for any reason the primary environment is unavailable. The secondary environment may lack some of the feedback and control features of the primary environment. However, it may be a more practical place for learning. The mechanism used to sort the identification of primary and secondary environments is an extension of the worksheet we used for displaying consequences—the Learning Environment Selection Worksheet shown in Figure 15. List all potential learning experiences for each major objective in the column so designated. Then, for each potential learning experience, define a primary and secondary learning environment. Using the operation of a forklift truck objective, the display would look as shown in Figure 15.

In the Figure 15 example, two of the primary environments are work locations, two others are reading stations, and one is an audio-visual center. The secondary environments include three real or simulated work locations and a classroom. In total, three of the five learning experiences can be accommodated at the work location, which has also been identified as the place of normal demonstration. It would seem that the primary learning environment for this objective would be the work location. However, such a designation would preclude use of two learning experiences. By going back to the analysis of presentation modes and applying the tests of operation, sophistication, and portability, we would come to the conclusion that the programmed instruction is portable and could be transported to the work location, if necessary. Not so with the videotape. There we have two choices: exclude it as a learning resource or identify a secondary location where the machine can be accessed.

By going through the process, the learning experience and the demonstration environment for each objective will be coordinated. The result is an identification of whether or not learning can be accommodated in the real world or if special environments need to be considered. For those objectives where the primary learning environment is different from the place of normal demonstration, construction of feedback and consequence mechanisms is needed to simulate those that exist in the real world. The guide to this is the Learning Environment Selection Worksheet.

Figure 15

Learning Environment Selection Worksheet

LEARNING ENVIRONMENT SELECTION WORKSHEET

Major Objective	Skills to Be Demonstrated	Normal Demonstration		Unique Consequences of Demonstration				Potential Learning Experiences	Learning Environment	
		Environment	Frequency	Correctly Performed		Incorrectly Performed			Primary	Secondary
				Short-term	Long-term	Short-term	Long-term			
Operate a forklift	1. Starting, driving, stopping	Warehouse stock room	Continuous	None	None	No or erratic movement	None	1. Trial & error	Work location	Simulated work location
	2. Manipulating fork	Warehouse stock room	Continuous	None	None	Stock damaged, topping	None	2. Guided instruction	Work location	Simulated work location
	3. Servicing	Maintenance room	Daily	Vehicle operator	None	Vehicle does not operate	None	3. Videotape	A/V center	Classroom
	4. Preventive Maintenance	Maintenance room	Weekly	None	Vehicle operator	None	Vehicle does not operate	4. Programmed instruction	Reading station	Classroom
								5. Operator's manual	Reading station	Work location

As each objective is charted, the pattern of the program will emerge. Some objectives will have primary learning environments in the real world. Others will require simulated environments, but overall, one environment or the other will dominate. The primary environment that emerges may not be the one that is most frequently identified. It might be, instead, that some objectives are more important than others, that the success of the program hinges on those objectives, and that, therefore, the needs of those objectives must be accommodated. These objectives, then, dictate the selection of learning environments to the exclusion of other factors.

To summarize, the definition of the environment is accomplished by following the six-step process. The first step, definition of objectives, provides a framework around which environmental definition is displayed. Definition of the potential learning experiences is the second step. This is accomplished by including rather than excluding experiences. Third, the entry criteria assumptions are specified. Focus of the assumptions is on identifying learner characteristics that will result in failure to either complete training or to use the skills after training. The fourth specification, the framework of activities theory, is the broadest. It decides whether decisions concerning objectives, sequence, pace, presentation mode, and evaluation are to be delegated to the learner. Specifications of consequence assumptions is the fifth step. The analysis includes identification of presence, frequency, and timing of consequences in the normal demonstration environment. Finally, the five preceding steps are brought together and summarized as the primary and secondary environments of learning are chosen.

The process of defining the environment is tedious but necessary work. In LCI, it is the environment that will guide the learner. Unless the designer fully understands the world into which the learner will be placed, he or she will not be able to make predictions. Prediction of stimuli and consequences allows the designer to build in cues and feedback systems that signal success or danger to the learner. Without these special, built-in mechanisms, the environment would be uncontrolled and learning would occur randomly. Learning does occur in real life, but it is often inefficient and incomplete. Our learning environments are intended to complement the natural environment by creating artificial cues, feedback, and consequences that focus and accelerate learning. To know what must be built, we must know what is missing and the effect an absent stimulus or consequence will have. The environmental specifications give us the knowledge with which learning experiences can be constructed.

V. Construct the Learning Experience

This is the "fun" part of the LCI project. All previous work begins to pay off as the pieces are put together in the formulation of learning experiences. As discussed in the section on the General LCI Model, for each objective there will be one or more learning experiences. Each learning experience consists of a stimulus for learning, a skill demonstration, a skill assessment, and a learning exercise. Collectively, the experiences will make up the learning program. It is here that the designer calls upon all prior research, knowledge of the subject and environment, and creativity to construct experiences that will generate learning.

Any single objective may consist of a number of tasks. A learning experience should be constructed for each task that can stand alone. These are typically considered sub-objectives to the main objective. The key determinant of whether or not a task can stand alone is whether or not its performance can be measured in isolation from other tasks that make up the major objectives. All tasks that can be independently measured require individual learning experiences. A learning experience for our purposes is any process that elicits a response that can be assessed and, when appropriate, provides mechanisms to alter the predictable behavior of an individual.

Each experience should be considered an outline or map of the activities that will result in learning. There are five elements that should be provided the learner in each experience. They are:

(a) the objective of the experience;
(b) the description of the activity;
(c) the measurements and standards used in assessing proficiency;
(d) a description of learning resources; and
(e) the time plan for the accomplishment.

The objective contains the natural or simulated stimuli for performance. The description of the activity establishes the natural or simulated skill demonstration and will normally specify the locus of the environment of performance. The measurements and standards provide for skill assessment, while the learning resources establish potential learning exercises available to the learner. The time plan provides a planning reference point for both learners and administrators. All of these elements relate back to the learning experience subsystem discussed earlier.

Shown in Figure 16 is a learning experience that was used in a management training program (Wydra, 1968, 1973).

The caption "Required Activity #72" briefly identifies the objective of the experience. It tells the learner that the learning experience will be one of inducting a new person into the organization. The tasks involved in the objectives are displayed in the section called "Activity Description." In general terms, the learner is told the topography of performance. There are five specific tasks included in the example objective. Specifically, these are: interview, select, orient, train a new employee, and keep a log of activities.

Knowledge of the environment drawn from the Learning Environment Selection Worksheet makes it highly probable that a vacancy will occur, that applicants will vie for the position, and that the eventual selectee will be a naive

Figure 16

Learning Experience, Allied Management Training Program

REQUIRED ACTIVITY #72: Personnel—Employee Induction
ACTIVITY DESCRIPTION:

    Interview, select, orient and train a new part time Grocery or Front End employee. Keep a log of the things you did and the things the new employee was able to do after you completed the process.

MEASUREMENT AND STANDARDS:

    Selection approved by the Store Manager.

    Orientation takes place during the new employee's first day on the job.

    All training accomplished, on the clock, during the employees first week on the job.

    New employee scores 85% or better on all Skill Quizzes related to his/her job.*

RESOURCES:

    Documents—

    District, Division policies and procedures related to selection, orientation and training of new hires

    Allied Self-Instruction courses listed below

    Magazine reprint—"I Can't Find Good People Anymore"

    Division Orientation Checklist (if available)

    Proctor and Gamble Self-Instruction booklet—"How to Train Others"

    SMI Store Manager's Guide 148—"Getting to know the new employee"

    SMI Store Manager's Guide 160—"Training Employees"

    SMI Store Manager's Guide 166—"Correcting Employees"

    SMI Store Manager's Guide 178—"Coaching Them Along—At Store Level"

    SMI Store Manager's Guide 197—"Recruiting, Selecting and Orientation of Checkstand Employees"

    SMI Store Manager's Guide 198—"Training Checkout Employees"

    SMI Store Manager's Guide 220—"The Relationship of the Store Manager to new, young, employees"

    People—

    Store Manager

    Personnel Manager

    Training Manager

TIME PLAN: Projected   Actual

    Beginning Date: _____   _____

    Completion Date: _____   _____

Reference Time for Trained Employee: Approximately 8 hours.

NOTES: * Training materials include:

Stock Clerks—	Cashiers—	Baggers—
"Stock-It"	"Check Cashing"	"Bag-It"
"Mark-It"	"Customer Relations"	"Courtesy"
"Changing Prices"	"Handling Money"	
"Bag-It"	"Handling Food Stamps"	
"Courtesy"	"Handling Coupons"	
	"Weighing Produce"	
	"Position, Amount, Control"	
	"Bag-It"	
	"Courtesy"	

---

performer. The activities of the learner are, therefore, constructed around the realities of the environment. Interview and selection have short-term consequences. Their results are immediately known. An interview results in an available candidate. A selection, subsequent job offer, and hire result in a new employee. Orientation and training, however, have long-term consequences. Consequences that are less easily measured, therefore, require that a log be initiated to track behaviors. To demonstrate competence in the induction process, a learner must perform in a set manner that is controlled by both natural and simulated consequences. These consequences would have been noted on the Learner Environment Selection Worksheet as an aid to learning experiences design.

Some learners in the program will have had experience in inducting new employees; others will not. Regardless of prior experience, they all need to demonstrate competence. Their competence is measured by the mechanism established for the task. The standard of acceptable versus unacceptable performance is also identified. The measurements are the acceptance of the position by an applicant, orientation during the first day on the job, training within the first week of employment, and ability of a new hire to perform a standardized test. The standards, on the other hand, are store manager approval of the selection and a score of 85 percent on the new hire test results. This means that the learner needs to know the selections that are likely to be approved by the store manager. These, of course, are dictated by the standards that are specified in the policy and procedure manuals of the organization. The ability of the new hire to perform is also detailed and can be gauged on new hire tests by the trainee without reference to an outside source. Therefore, all measurements and standards are trainee interpretable. The learner is in control.

Those learners who cannot perform will need to acquire

additional skills. They need to enter a learning experience. The resources for learners in the learning exercise are listed in the section captioned "Resources." Not every learner will utilize these resources, nor will most learners use every resource. However, all resources that are available to all learners are listed so that the learner can decide on his or her own presentation mode.

There are two types of resources in this example, documents and people. This segregation of resources was made to give special recognition to the human resources for learning that exist in the environment. The learner, at his or her option, can access any or all of the resources to gain the required skills.

The final section shown in the example is the time plan. Here the learner is given a standard time, or the time it would take a trained performer to demonstrate the skill. The learner is asked to project how long it will take to demonstrate performance. An experienced performer will approximate the standard time, while a naive performer will schedule more time for the exercise. In any case, the learner makes a performance projection on his or her timing that will become a performance commitment. The recording of the actual time acts as a feedback mechanism to the learner on the accuracy of the projection.

The example identifies several key points in the construction of a learning experience. The major point to keep in mind is that the format is a diagram of learning performance. It needs to be complete but concise. It needs to contain all information needed by the learner which incorporates all controls planned by the designer.

In addition, it illustrates the vital point that the learning experience is learner oriented. It reflects all elements that the designer knows about the environment that will influence progress toward the objective. In the Potential Learning Experiences column of the Learning Environment Selection

Worksheet, the designer identified a variety of situations in which learning could occur. As the learning experience is constructed, the designer constricts the options of the learner by restricting the available alternatives. The constriction of the alternatives limits the directions that the learner can pursue. However, it increases the probability of accurate prediction on the part of the designer.

The potential learning experiences were developed as alternatives. It is in the specified experience that the potential is utilized. First, the most appropriate potential is used as the basis for design of the exercise. Typically, it will be the experience that fits the primary environment while giving maximum learning opportunity. Second, the remaining potential experiences incorporated into the resources pool can be selected as alternates by the learner. Keep in mind, however, that only those experiences that can be utilized by the learner should be included in the resources pool. Some experiences will require equipment, materials, personnel, or locations that are not available to the learner. As designers, we must recognize these shortcomings and eliminate the experience from the resources pool.

Each element of the learning experience presents its own special problems. The preparatory work of research, analysis, and specification accomplished in previous tasks will, in a large part, assist in the resolution of the problem. With these points in mind, a quick review of each of the parts of a learning experience is useful.

(a) The Objective of the Experience

The objective in a learning experience is written for learner comprehension. The two major areas of concern in writing a learning experience objective are scope and vagueness. The tendency of some designers is to make the objective too broad.

The scope of the experience becomes so large that it could

be considered a program in itself. To aid the learner, the scope of each experience should be limited to one unified task. By doing this, the measurement tool can be specifically tailored to measure end results. Vagueness is also a problem. What seems clear and concise to the designer is sometimes less than clear to the learner. Well-defined action verbs that succinctly transfer the designer's meaning of what is to be accomplished should consistently be used. As an aid to avoiding both excessive scope and vagueness, use the Learning Environment Selection Worksheet. It lists all of the elements of a good objective. It also limits activities to a single task and focuses on actions, environments, and consequences, all of which will be useful to you.

(b) The Description of the Activity

The description of the activity guides learner behavior while he or she is accomplishing the objective. The problem most commonly encountered here is over-specification. Yes, the learner needs guidance if he or she is to be directed to an end-result without a coach, but room must be left for the creative exploration of the learner. Secondly, if the topography of the behavior is too constricted, it may discourage behaviors that would validly meet the end-result objective.

(c) The Measurements and Standards
Used in Assessing Proficiency

The primary problem of establishing measurements and standards is the frequent absence of an adequate measurement tool. It is here that the creativity of the designer is most frequently challenged. What measurements are used to evaluate the comprehension of a theory or the visual discrimination between two similar objects? Once measured, what is the standard of acceptable performance? The difficulty, of course, arises because in LCI we substitute objective measures for subjective judgments. The measurement tools are placed in the hands of the learner, and he or she is told, DECIDE. To allow that decision, the designer will need to probe the subject matter expert's rationale. The decision-making points need clarification and crystallization. These should be stated in such a way that the naive learner will be able to comprehend just how performance will be measured.

(d) A Description of Learning Resources

In preparing learning resources, the problem will be one of relevance. With an adequately researched task, there will be a wealth of resources. Resources were categorized as the environment was defined. In the research of potential learning experiences, alternatives surfaced. As the research and analysis developed, it was highly probable that additional resources were added to the list. The task during those stages was inclusion, not exclusion. Now, however, the task is exclusion. The stage was set for exclusion as the decisions to be delegated were categorized. General rules were established for the exclusion of resources. Nonetheless, you will still have a variety of resources that have survived the purge. As the learning experience is prepared, these must be restricted further, and here the major test of inclusion is relevance. Resources that do not address the conditions imposed in the objectives, activities, and measurements must be refined to provide maximum utility to the learner. Information maps may be necessary to route learners through a book, or chapter, or page. Videotapes and audiotapes may need to be cued. Graphics may need to be cropped. The aim is to focus the learning to eliminate irrelevancies. The difficulty in all this will be to strike a balance between elimination and retention of resources. The learner needs variety of resources, but not at the price of irrelevance.

(e) The Time Plan for the Accomplishment

The final problem in establishing learning exercises is in establishing the time frame for performance. The probability is high that there will be little or no reliable data available detailing the time needed to execute a performance. How long does it take a master performer to recruit a job candidate, and interview, orient, and train him or her? How long does it take for a driver to park a car? Two hours? Two minutes? Thirty seconds? The duration of the normal time length of performance is frequently not recorded. But the learner needs the data so that projections about both performance and learning time can be made. Since the learner in LCI may plan, pace, sequence, and decide other variables, he or she needs projected data on how long the tasks will take. He or she is a naive performer. The time data is not in his or her experience bank. The designer, therefore, will need to research the subject to provide a framework within which time planning can take place.

Summary

The construction of the learning experience is a creative exercise for the designer. All research is synthesized into an exercise that will stimulate a demonstration of behavior. If the behavior is outside of the learner's repertoire, the resources that can be used for learning are marshaled and used. The end-result of entry into a learning exercise is a trained person, but the creativity of the designer is not haphazard. It draws upon the prior research and analysis that have been done, and it focuses on eliciting predictable resources from naive performers. General guidance and direction are balanced against over-specificity of action. While the designer predicts the end, the means are left largely to the learner.

In the process of design, problem areas will be encountered. The problems are inherent to the nature of the task.

Here, too, the designer draws upon his or her creativity to remove frustrations from the path of the learner. Because of the nature of many of these problems, even more research may be needed to resolve them. Nevertheless, it is the task of the designer to do the research that will facilitate learning. If that takes extra research, it is simply the price of an effective learning experience.

VI. Validate the Design

Of all the concepts introduced into instructional technology over the past half century, the concept of validation has had the most profound effect. It is the embodiment of the scientific method. This application of the scientific method to instruction has raised the process of instruction from an art to a technology. Yet, validation is a task that is often sloppily handled or even omitted from the instructional design process.

Mothers love their children, even if they turn out badly. Instructional designers love their programs, even if they don't instruct. Mothers are often reluctant to cut loose the apron strings so that the child can learn from the harsh reality of experience; so too are designers. Perhaps it is the link to artistry that makes designers reluctant to *test* the results of their programs against the promise. Whatever the reason, the omission of validation is nowhere more dangerous than in LCI. In conventional designs, the instructor is present to alter decisions and to make new decisions to compensate for design error. Not so in LCI. The learner, the naive learner, is in charge, and he or she will in all probability not have the knowledge or skill to change a poor design. Therefore, a design that allows a massive individual investment and yet fails to accomplish the objective is, at best, a hoax.

It is incumbent upon the designer to insure that his or her program is not a hoax and that it will produce the predicted outcome. The only way to make such a guarantee is to validate the program.

The concept of validation is a powerful one. It is directly linked with the measurement devices of competency-based learning and instructor accountability. It tests the learning program hypothesis. If the hypothesis is valid, the specified learning occurs. *Should the specified learning fail to occur, the program must be revised.* Too often, instead of changing the program, the designer changes the objective to match the results that have been produced. In other words, the prediction is changed *after* the fact. At best, this approach is sloppy. At worst, it fails in aiding the technologist in learning the effect of certain techniques and assumes a consistency of results that may be more illusion than fact. On the other hand, revision of the program until it produces the predicted results places the burden of "teaching" on the program, which is where it belongs. In 1958, B.F. Skinner wrote in *Science* magazine that "Difficult as programming is, it has its compensations. It is a salutary thing to try to guarantee a right response at every step in the presentation of a subject matter."

The validation process is neither mysterious nor complex, but it *is* time-consuming. This single drawback is often the excuse given for its omission. Validation procedures range from individual tryouts involving designer observation of learning behaviors and results to group tryouts where responses and results are statistically analyzed. In all cases, simple and complex, there are four basic tasks included in the validation process:

1. Specify the Outcome (prediction).
2. Apply the Learning Process.
3. Measure the Outcome (actual).
4. Compare Prediction to Actual Outcomes.

The comparison is the key step in validation. However, the comparison can be questioned if the preceding steps are not technically sound. If the specifications of outcomes are vague, or if the learning process application is contaminated, or if the outcome measurement is inconsistent or unreliable, the process will be flawed. Any of these will invalidate the comparison of actual to predicted outcomes, even though there appears to be a perfect match. If the validation process is sound, the comparison of actual to predicted results will determine whether program revision is necessary. A program in which actual results consistently match predictions is a validated program. It fulfills the promise. Programs that do not pass the validation process need revision. Programs must be tested, revised, and tested again until there is a match. The failure of a program to validate on the first test is no dishonor to the designer. The only dishonor is when a program that fails to validate is put into use.

In LCI, individual rather than group testing appears to be more practical. This does not, however, preclude putting a group into the program and then following up on individuals. In fact, this may be necessary if learner interactions are an assumed element in the environment. However, the complexity of the design and the opportunity for random learner behavior argue against attempting to make initial assessments solely on the basis of group statistics.

Individual testing will involve monitoring the movement of one or more individuals through the program. In an extended time length program, it will mean checking their behavior, while noting on a daily basis their interaction with the environment, and output. The designer's propensity will be to interact with them and to clarify ambiguities—don't. Such interaction will contaminate the learning process. If the designer in the role of validator or evaluator will not be on site while future learners use the program, don't muddy up the results of the test by interjecting his or her presence into the environment. In most cases, the designer will not be a resource to future learners, so he or she should not act like one in the testing environment. Karen Brethower (1965) suggests some useful guidelines for individual testing that are applicable in the LCI mode:

1. Minimize verbal instruction to individual test subjects.
2. Set a standard procedure for your own behavior in administering the program and follow up rigorously.
3. If it is necessary to give instruction during the testing of the program, have it be written rather than verbal. In this way, you will have a record of what was added.
4. Tape record the procedure. You will have a record of what was said and will learn about the teaching you are doing quite aside from what the program is teaching.

To these can be added four additional guidelines that would have particular application to the LCI mode of instruction:

1. Be inconspicuous. You are not expected to be a part of the environment, therefore, do not interject yourself.
2. Do not offer value judgments on learner performance. The learner is there to learn and not to please you.
3. Do not make notations on learner material. If necessary, make a photostatic or photographic copy of a document to hold your comments, but retain the unblemished integrity of the learner's materials.
4. Use what you collect to improve your program for its next test.

The observation of these guidelines will not guarantee a validated program on the next try, but it will reduce the risk that an apparently validated program is, in fact, invalid.

Too many times, the lessons of a tryout or even actual field experience are not implemented because the program has been cast in concrete—or at least in printer's ink. It is awfully difficult to justify revisions to a program—even if that program doesn't work—after large sums of money have been spent on artwork, photography, printing, films, and packaging. Imagine, if you will, dumping an instructional segment costing thousands of dollars to produce simply because it is either irrelevant to the objective or fails to accomplish its missions. Few instructional designers are secure enough in their craft to insist on such an action. The alternative is, of course, to validate before, rather than after, the finished material is produced. As elementary as this may seem, it is often overlooked. The rule is: "don't print before you prove."

By putting the program through a rigorous validation process, the designer will be confident in making predictions about its utility. Test, where possible, each assumption. When the population was defined in terms of demographics, subculture, and capability, were the assumptions and projections valid? What proof was there? The "required" performance results were defined. Were those results really required? What proof was there? The learning environment and the learning objectives, potential learning experiences, and the entry criteria were defined. Were they correct? Again, what proof is there? Can the positions taken be defended? Point after point, the program requires validation until finally the validation process itself must be held up to examination. It is then that the designer knows if, in the process of proving the points, the process has been comprised. A virtuous designer, rare creature indeed, of a LCI program will have at least a chance for success as measured by learner results.

VII. Package the Program

Now, the bits, the pieces are all there. The strategy is in place. The tactics work. The program has been conceived, nurtured, and it has proven its promise. All that remains is to put a bow on it. It needs to be packaged. At this point, it would be easy to turn the entire project over to another and say, "Pack it up for delivery." Don't do it. The packaging needs to be managed with the same care that has been given to the development of the program. The package is the visual and intellectual stimulus that will have an impact on the learner. It must be attractive; yes, and it must be functional. Most important, it must be organized.

At this point, only the designer knows how the trainee will interact with the materials. The designer can guess at the routes a learner will take, the associations the learner will make. The designer knows the learner's language, communication, strengths, and weaknesses. All of these may be important in putting the program together in a package that will attract and not repel the learner. Color, typeface, and size of material all make visual impact upon the learner. The color, sizes, and types need to be organized so that they have meaning to the learner, and so that they will aid in the accessing of materials. While the designer will not be a part of the learning environment, the learning materials will. Their presence can be used to advantage by insuring that they stimulate entry and exploration rather than impede it.

One LCI program I came into contact with was simply a mimeographed learner's guide and assorted references. The learner left the orientation with arms heaped full of materials. References not having the good fortune to have come from a publisher were casually stapled together. Sometimes, the faintly reproduced pages were inverted, out of sequence, or even omitted. The audiotapes were labeled by numbers rather than name. Two, three, and more references were made on a tape without an index. Books were provided as resources when only paragraphs, unmarked paragraphs at that, were to be accessed. In other words, the packaging of the program was disorganized. When I talked with the designer, he told me of a program that was elegant in its simplicity. When I talked with a learner, he told me of the frustrations imposed upon him because of the complexity of the learning process. Both were accurate in their perceptions. The program was elegantly simple; it was also outrageously complex. The simplicity of design was obscured by the disorganization of the resources. When we revised the packaging of materials to make them more easily accessible, visually coordinated, and organizationally integrated, the learner's perception was revised to match that of the designer. The content was not changed, but its presentation was. The tangible effect of the reorganization was a small, but significant, reduction in overall learning time and a decrease in the learner-initiated drop-out rate.

Again, the essential element is aiding the learner. Any element of packaging that aids the learner is useful. Elements that do not are irrelevant.

Summary of Design Process

The design process of the LCI model began with an exploration of the application of the general model. The general model processed a naive learner through a learning environment to produce a trained learner. The design process consists of seven discrete steps, some more complex than others but all important.

The definition of the mission established the overall or broad task that the program would address. It established the framework of the objectives and imposed relevant constraints.

Next, the target population was defined. This included an analysis of the probable population using demographics, subculture, and capability analyses. These analytical tools aided in the categorization of learning groups. The demographic analysis gave insight into the probable behaviors of the learner based on what we know about how groups of people sharing certain characteristics will behave. The subculture analysis reviewed behavior predictions based upon the environment from which the learner was drawn. Lastly, the capability analysis categorized individual skills and deficiencies that would aid or impair learning.

The third step was to define the required performance results. Here the designer developed the mission statement to the next level of specificity based upon what was learned about the learner. These requirements were developed into performance statements that specified what the learner should be able to do, under what conditions, and to what degree.

Definition of the environmental specifications followed. Noting that the environment is the key resource in the program, the steps of environmental specification included specifying major learning objectives, potential learning experiences, entry criteria assumptions, the framework of activities theory, the consequence assumptions, and the environmental assumptions. The issues of objectives, sequencing, pacing, presentation mode, and evaluation were addressed within the theory of the framework of activities. The consequence assumptions developed techniques for the analyzing of those forces that will have an impact on the learner within the learning environment. The short-term and long-term impacts of performance were explained as guides to how the consequences could or could not be used to steer learning. Finally, the definition of the environment required the designer to make explicit his or her assumptions about that environment. At this stage, the designer also identified the potential learning experiences that could be employed to facilitate learning and the primary and secondary environments in which these experiences occur.

The fifth step in the design process was to construct the learning experience. Here the elements of individual experience objectives, descriptions of activities, measurements and standards, learning resources, and time plans were developed as guides for learners.

The learning experience was organized by placing it in a format that will facilitate learning. The elements of activity description, measurements and standards, and resources were identified for the learner in a predetermined pattern to allow concentration on the content of instruction and not on its process.

In the last two steps, the preliminary design was formatted, and the program was validated and packaged. All tasks were focused on access and integrity from the viewpoint of the learner. The preliminary design established a road map to allow learner navigation through the program. The validation allowed the designer to predict and, with some assurance, guarantee results. The final package tied the total effort together so that it will be an adequate stimulus for learning.

The overall design process is one of rigorous work and intense analysis. It is the application of a technical knowledge to a learning problem. Where facts exist, they are used. Where discriminations or generalizations can be made that will aid the learner in managing his or her own learning effort, they are used. The entire thrust is to use what we know about learning to allow learning to occur. All this is done without the artificial constraints that may aid teaching but not necessarily learning. The key to this design process is, of course, the development of measurement tools that will allow both specification of objectives and evaluation of results. When these measurements are in place, environments can be discovered or constructed to facilitate learning which is controlled by the learner and which is more efficient and effective than instructor controlled instruction.

References

Brethower, K.S. *University of Michigan Center for Programmed Learning, Occasional Paper No. V.,* 1965.

Creative Universal, Inc. *Sherwin Williams Store Management Development Program,* in use at the Sherwin Williams Company, Cleveland, 1975.

Horn, R.F. *et al. A Reference Collection of Rules and Guidelines for Writing Information Mapped Materials.* Information Resources, Inc., 1971.

Knowles, M.S. *The Modern Practice of Adult Education.* New York: Association Press, 1970.

Mager, R.F. *Preparing Instructional Objectives.* Belmont, California: Fearon Publishers, 1962.

Rousseau, J.J. *Emile,* 1762.

Skinner, B.F. *Science,* 1958.

Skinner, B.F. *Beyond Freedom and Dignity.* New York: Alfred A. Knopf, 1971.

United States Air Force. *Handbook for Designers of Instruction Systems: Planning, Developing, and Validating Instruction.* Washington, D.C.: July 15, 1973.

Warren, M. *Training for Results.* New York: Addison-Wesley, 1969.

Wydra, F.T. *Store Management Training Program,* in use at Allied Supermarkets, Inc., Detroit, 1968.

Wydra, F.T. "Learner Controlled Workshop," Detroit: ASTD Detroit Institute Day Presentation, 1973.

VII.

RESOURCES

Blitz, B. *The Open Classroom. Making It Work.* Boston: Allyn and Bacon, 1973.

Bruner, J. (Ed.) *Learning About Learning: A Conference Report 1963.* U.S. Department of Health, Education, and Welfare, U.S. Government Printing Office, Washington, DC, 1966.

Combs, A.W. *Educational Accountability.* Association for Supervision and Curriculum Development, Washington, DC, 1972.

David, T.G. *Learning Environments.* Illinois: University of Chicago Press, 1975.

Davis, R.H. *Learning System Design.* New York: McGraw-Hill, 1974.

Gentile, J.R. *Instructional Applications of Behavior Principles.* Montery, California: Brooks/Cole Publishing Company, 1973.

Green, E.J. *The Learning Process and Programmed Instruction.* New York: Holt, Rinehart, and Winston, 1962.

Hook, S. *Education and the Taming of Power.* LaSalle, Illinois: Open Court Publishing Company, 1973.

Hume, E.G. *Learning and Teaching in the Infant's School.* New York: Longmans, Green, 1952.

Kaufman, R. *Need Assessment.* University Consortium for Instructional Development and Technology, San Diego, California, 1975.

Kohl, H.R. *The Open Classroom.* New York: Random House, 1969.

Malott, R.W. *et al. Contingency Management in Education.* Kalamazoo, Michigan: Behaviordelia, 1972.

Malott, R.W. *et al.* (Eds.) *An Introduction to Behavior Modification.* Kalamazoo, Michigan: Behaviordelia, 1973.

Nilsson, N.J. *Learning Machines.* New York: McGraw-Hill, 1965.

Pearson, N.P. *Learning Resource Centers.* Minneapolis: Burgess Publishing Company, 1973.

Rowell, J. *Educational Media Selection Centers.* Chicago: American Library Association, 1971.

Sabaroff, R., and M.A. Hanna. *The Open Classroom.* Metuchen, New Jersey: Scarecrow Press, Inc., 1974.

Schwitzgebel, R.K., and D.A. Kolb. *Changing Human Behavior.* New York: McGraw-Hill, 1974.

Shirley-Smith, K. *Programmed Learning in Integrated Industrial Training.* London: Gower Press, 1968.

Spodek, B., and H.J. Walberg. *Studies in Open Education.* New York: Schochen Books, 1975.

Thomas, J. *Learning Centers.* Boston: Holbrook Press, 1976.

Toffler, A. *Learning for Tomorrow.* New York: Random House, 1974.

Walsh, W.B. *Theories of Person-Environment Interaction.* The American College Testing Program, Pennsylvania, 1973.

Wilson, L. *The Open Access Curriculum.* Boston: Allyn and Bacon, 1971.

Wilson, S.R., and D.T. Tosti. *Learning Is Getting Easier.* San Rafael, California: Individual Learning Systems, 1972.

FRANK T. WYDRA is Vice President of Human Resources for Harper-Grace Hospitals of Detroit, Michigan. In his current position, he is responsible for all personnel plans and programs of one of the nation's leading hospital organizations. Mr. Wydra was previously Vice President of Personnel for Allied Supermarkets, Inc., and has held a variety of staff and operating positions during his career. The keystone of his efforts has been the application of behavioral technology in industrial organizations. An early practitioner of the programmed learning process, he has been responsible for the adoption of self-instruction as the primary basic skills training tool in organizations he has served. Mr. Wydra is a frequent speaker at management and professional conferences. He is a graduate of the University of Illinois and an active member of the Training Research Forum (TRF) and the American Society for Training and Development. He has been active in the National Society for Performance and Instruction (NSPI) at both the chapter and national levels. In 1974, he was given the NSPI Award for Contribution to the Technology, and in 1975 he received the ASTD National Torch Award for the introduction of the Concept of LCI to industry.